Just the

FAQ*s

about

GOD

* Frequently Asked Questions

NELSON

Book design and composition by Robin Crosslin
Illustrations by Doug Cordes

Just the FAQs about God
ISBN 0-7852-4761-0

Printed in the United States of America

1 2 3 4 5 6 7 – 07 06 05 04 03 02

FAQ #1

 How Does God Explain the Existence of the Universe?

 Every effect must have an adequate cause, and God is the only cause adequate for the existence of the universe.

Only in the last 100 years or so have modern peoples believed that the universe was not created by supernatural power. With the theory of evolution, intelligent people were able believe an explanation for the universe that didn't require a God. But evolutionists still have to explain where the universe came from, and they have only two choices. One, God created the universe; or, two, the universe came into existence by itself. If you believe the latter, you must also believe that the universe was caused by nothing, or that the stuff that the universe came from has always existed and designed itself by chance.

"I can see how it might be possible for a man to look down upon the earth and be an atheist, but I cannot conceive how he could look up into the heavens and say there is no God."

Abraham Lincoln

Let's look at the viewpoint that matter is eternal; it has always been here. After an indeterminable length of time, this matter simmered, cooked, boiled, and finally exploded in one great big bang. Matter began flying out to the far corners of the universe, cooled, and formed suns, stars, planets, and moons.

On our own planet, things simmered, cooked, boiled, and pretty soon life began, for no reason, in primitive forms. Life eventually evolved into plants, animals, and human beings; all through random chance, evolutionary scientists say. It's all one great big happy accident. But there are several flaws with that explanation.

First, scientific evidence doesn't support it adequately. If you believe the evolutionary big bang theory together with evolution, then, as Francis Schaeffer, an evangelical theologian and scholar of the last generation, used to say, you are locked into the equation: "nothing + the impersonal + time + chance = everything there is." The problem is, science itself doesn't support that conclusion, indeed it can't support it until that process can be observed. How can something come from nothing? How can the personal come from the impersonal? How can the intricacy, the design, the order, and the symmetry be a product of chance?

Ancient False Theories

In Western civilization there are three common historical alternatives to believing in the existence of God.

1. Atheism: the belief that God does not exist.

2. Agnosticism: the belief that you cannot know God even if He does exist.

3. Pantheism: the belief that all forces and objects in the universe are God. Rocks, trees, animals, the earth, and humankind—all are part of God.

Present-Day False Theories

Added to that list are two modern alternatives to disbelieving God's existence.

1. The New Age Movement: This movement has been characterized by a general reliance on pantheism, paganism, reincarnation, and the revival of the supernatural.

2. Secular Theology: Though this term is inherently contradictory, nevertheless, there are those who work within churches and/or denominations who, in spite of that incongruity, do not believe in God as the Bible describes Him.

Second, it violates science. In his book *The Church at the End of the Twentieth Century*, Schaeffer tells about Murray Eden at MIT. Eden was working with a high-speed computer to answer this question: "Beginning with chaos at any acceptable amount of time up to eight billion years ago, could the present complexity of the universe come about by chance?" The answer was absolutely "No." And few scientists think the earth is older than eight billion years. Four to four-and-a-half billion years is commonly accepted. More recently, the British scientist Sir Fred Hoyle, a mathematician and astronomer, calculated that it would take ten to the forty thousandth power years ($10^{40,000}$) for chance to produce even the simplest cell. That length of time is unimaginable, so much older than the present universe is thought to be, that it discounts any possibility that the big bang and evolution caused our universe.

God created the universe.

Of course, the big bang theory, as an astronomical theory, is not inherently tied to the biological theory of evolution. In fact, some Christians believe that the big bang theory accurately describes what happened when God created the universe. Nevertheless, much discussion of the big bang theory is linked to the theory of biological evolution, and vice-versa, as if biological evolution were merely a logical continuation of the big bang.

Do you want me to believe that something came from nothing? Or that matter is eternal and that everything there came about by chance? You may be willing to believe that, but I am not. It is no greater stretch of faith to believe in God than to believe in other "causes" for the universe. Whenever you see something, you are driven backwards to ask, "Who created it?" When you get to original matter, you must ask the same. At that point, if you stop and say, "No one created it. It is eternal. It has always been there."—or if you say that "nothing" was in the beginning and that therefore something came from nothing—

that isn't an adequate explanation of cause and effect.

If I say, "God created the matter," my inquisitive friends will usually say, "Aha! But who created God?" As though they had me. Not so. There has to be an starting point. You must start with something, or else something has come from nothing, which is nonsense. The question is, do you want to stop with a big ball of mud bubbling in the center of the universe and say that everything in our world is a result of an explosion in that big ball? Do you want to stop the whole discussion by saying, "The big ball just always was?" Or, do you want to stop with an eternal Being who has always existed and will always exist, who is powerful and intelligent beyond our capacity to comprehend? You must stop with a great ball of mud, or you must stop with God. Which will it be? Stopping with God takes no more faith and answers more questions.

E**very cause has its effect**

FAQ #2

How Does God Explain the Order and Purpose in the Universe?

The order and purpose in the universe suggest an intelligent creator behind it.

Not only is the universe "here," and therefore to be accounted for, but its order, design, and purpose must also be accounted for. It is the difference between all the parts of a watch lying in a jumbled heap on a table and having it up and running on your wrist. It is one thing to explain where the jumble of parts came from. It is quite another thing to explain how they all got put together in such a way as to tell time. Not only is the universe "here" but it also runs like a precision watch.

What we used to call matter is beginning to look more and more as if it is not merely matter but little compressed balls of energy. If this is true, then the universe is held together by an amazing power indeed!

Many evolutionists want to believe in the big bang and evolution theories, not because the evidence is overwhelming, but because, in their minds, beginning with an bias against God, there is no other acceptable alternative.

Sir Fred Hoyle, a highly regarded British scientist, wrote in an article entitled "The Big Bang in Astronomy":

Brain Stretcher

As philosophers and theologians debate the existence of God, they break the arguments into two categories with these names:

Naturalistic Arguments

1. Cosmological Argument (cosmos = the universe; logos = study of). The universe exists. God explains the fact that there is "something rather than nothing."

2. Teleological Argument (teleos = purpose; logos = study of). The universe has remarkable order, suggesting intelligence and design behind it. God explains the order and apparent design in the universe.

3. Anthropological Argument (anthropos = man; logos = study of). Man is unique in all of creation. He longs to know who he is, where he came from, why he is here, where he is going. God explains the uniqueness of humanity in creation.

Biblical Argument

The Bible is true to what is. Explanations of reality in the Bible conform to the conclusions suggested by the naturalistic arguments. Thus, the naturalistic arguments and the biblical record affirm each other.

The latest data differ by so much from what theories would suggest as to kill the big bang cosmologies, but now because the scientific world is enamored by the big bang theory, the facts are ignored (*The New Scientist*, p. 521).

Robert Jastro, the well-known geologist, physicist, and agnostic, wrote:

Perhaps the appearance of life on earth is a miracle. Scientists are reluctant to accept that view, but their choices are limited. Either life was created on earth by a being outside the grasp of scientific understanding, or it evolved on our planet spontaneously through chemical reactions in non-living matter lying on the surface of the planet. The first theory places the question of the origin of life beyond the reach of scientific inquiry. It is a statement of faith in the power of a supreme being not subject to the laws of science. The second theory is also an act of faith. The act of faith consists in assuming that the scientific view of origins is correct without having any evidence to support that belief ("God's Creation," p. 68).

Order testifies to intelligence.

Scientists do not reject creation because the evidence demands it, but because their approach to science will not allow them to allow God's existence as the beginning point for understanding the universe and life. Thus God or the big bang and evolution theories appear to be their only alternatives. Were they to approach the data with a will open to the existence and consequences of God's reality, many more of them would find that God alone satisfactorily explains what we observe in the universe.

FAQ #3

 How Does God Explain the Uniqueness of Humanity?

 Humankind is a higher being than all other animals, and being created in the image of God explains why.

Humans are different from animals, and ancient cave drawings suggest that people have always considered themselves different. Man longs to know who he is, where he came from, where he is going. He longs for purpose and meaning. This difference is explained because man is made in the image of God.

Man has a conscience, a moral sense of right and wrong, superior intelligence, and sense of a spiritual domain. He believes that some things are right and wrong. He feels guilty when he does what he thinks is wrong. These are not mere evolutionary developments. They are special capaci-

Why I need to know arguments for the existence of God

1. To avoid falling into ancient false belief systems already identified and discredited in church history.

2. To avoid being deceived by a present-day cult or false religion.

3. To strengthen my own faith and walk with God.

4. To be able to speak intelligently about God with others.

ties given to man by God, who has not given them to animals. Pigs don't commit suicide out of despair over the meaninglessness of life. Kangaroos don't revolt against their superiors because of discrimination in the herd. Buffalo never draw crude sketches of themselves on a cave wall.

Humans are different from non-humans. They are higher than the animals. They are superior, not just in the quality and quantity of their intelligence, but also in their spiritual nature. One century of atheism is about all the atheism you can find in history, and it is on its way out as a dominating cultural force.

Humanity differs from the animals.

When the Soviet Union, a bastion of atheism, disintegrated, the church in the former Soviet republics grew. The church in China at the time of this writing is repressed but continues to grow. In the United States, there is a dramatic revival of religion, though much of it is not Christian. The time may come when, as a society, we may look back on atheism and say, "How profoundly short-sighted and narrow-minded!"

God made us superior to the animals and intended us to live accordingly. The more humanity forgets God, the more people will act like mere animals. But unlike animals, people have the capacity to change.

FAQ #4

 How Does Biblical Evidence Demand the Existence of God?

 The Bible concurs with our observations about life and the universe, and describes the God who made it.

We have not begun by looking at the Bible to answer our wondering about the existence of God. If we had, you might have objected that appealing first to the Bible is like asking someone on trial to be his own character witness. On the other hand, you would expect the Bible to concur with reality.

The Bible affirms our looking at the universe for initial evidence for the existence of God:

The heavens declare the glory of God; and the firmament shows His handiwork (Psalm 19:1).

O LORD, our Lord, how excellent is Your name in all the earth, who have set Your glory above the heavens! When I consider Your heavens, the work of Your fingers, the moon and the stars, which You have ordained, what is man that You are mindful of him, and the son of man that You visit him? O LORD, our Lord, how excellent is Your name in all the earth! (Psalm 8:1, 3, 4, 9).

The Bible proclaims that the universe reveals God.

God intended the intricacy and design of the universe to point to Him. Concerning that intention, Romans 1:18–20 reads,

For the wrath of God is revealed from heaven against all ungodliness and unrighteousness of men, who suppress the truth in unrighteousness, because what may be known of God is manifest in them, for God has shown it to them. For since the creation of the world His invisible attributes are clearly seen, being understood by the things that are made, even His eternal power and Godhead, so that they are without excuse.

Concerning the uniqueness of humanity, the Bible says in Genesis 1:26 and 27 that God made man in His image and likeness, male and female.

The Bible's consistent witness that God exists and the naturalistic arguments we have considered together amply justify believing in God.

God is found through an appropriate search.

If you have for some reason already decided that you do not want to believe in God, then you can devise evidence to support your decision. Deciding that you won't believe in God is like deciding ahead of time that you don't have cancer, and therefore, you explain away all the evidence that might suggest that you do. Yet what you think about whether or not you have cancer is irrelevant. What is relevant is whether or not you have it. Therefore, the only safe course of action is to look at all the evidence and be willing to modify your initial decision when you find the evidence compelling.

If all this were merely a matter of intellectual curiosity, we could debate it until we ran out of energy, ended in a stalemate, shrugged our shoulders and said, "Well, that was interesting, but I guess there's no way to know for sure." Then we could go home and think about something else.

But it is certainly more than an intellectual debate to me. I want to know if there is a God. I want to know if it is safe to die, I want to know if there is something I can do to make everything okay for me when they lay me six feet under and throw a shovel full of dirt in my face.

I also want to know if it is safe to live. I want to know if there is purpose and meaning in life now. I want to know if I am going through life on my own, at the mercy of random blows of fate, or if there is a God who loves me and will guide me and look out for me. I want to know if there is someone I can pray to, or if I am alone. I want to know if there is such a thing as truth and error, right and wrong. When I lose my job, when my family falls apart, when my health fails, when the wrong person is elected, or my town is ravaged by a flood, is there a God? Will He see me through the trials of life?

I'm not going to jeopardize my eternal destiny or present sense of meaning and purpose in life by deciding ahead of time that there is no God, and then interpret all the evidence in light of that presupposition, without searching for God in ways appropriate to such a search. If you want to learn of or know God, you must search for Him in a way that leads to Him.

Here we identify a few crucial characteristics of any good-faith effort to know God and thus to fully consider "all the evidence." The God who created the universe and with the breathtaking diversity of plant and animal life we can observe—this God is, at the least, the supremely intelligent, creative, and powerful Being of the universe. The Bible consistently witnesses to this. He communicates with His creation and desires an ongoing, authentic relationship with humanity.

How do these characteristics of God help us know how we should approach Him? If God is, He is a Being whom we should approach only with the highest respect and in the most profound humility. Only when people approach Him in humility, seeking to know Him on His terms, in His way, can they claim to have examined all the evidence concerning His existence.

If you do not know God or haven't yet made up your mind about His existence, don't stop your inquiry before bending your knee in honor to Him and in humility before Him, asking Him to make Himself known to you. If the prospect of approaching God in this way repulses you, at least you know that there's more to this inquiry than a cool, detached, impersonal sifting of evidence: You have bumped into the main reason people don't believe in God—their wills.

Julian Huxley confessed that his scientist colleagues embraced evolutionary theory so quickly because it did not challenge their morality, while the God of the Bible certainly did. If we see that the naturalistic and biblical evidence makes the existence of God plausible, but we still resist acknowledging or bowing before Him, we should face the true source of our resistance—not external facts (or a lack of facts), but our internal will. We are unwilling to give ourselves over to Him, which is what He requires of those who would know Him. Repentance and obedience are the key elements in a search for God,

Repentance and obedience are the key elements in a search for God.

and these actions destroy our autonomy and freedom from ultimate accountability. So naturally we resist bending the knee. But that is finally the only way we can really both know that God exists and know him.

And, ironically, when we do find God we discover that it was He who found us. Apart from God's grace, we don't want to know Him. He places in our hearts the desire to know Him. He leads us in our search. When we come to love God, we discover that it was He who first loved us.

THINKING BACK

Do you want to know God? That is exciting. It indicates that God Himself, the Creator of the universe, is knocking on the door of your life. In a spirit of repentance and obedience, let Him in. Tell Him that you believe in Him fully. Tell Him that you are willing to repent of your sins and that you want Him to come into your life and help you to become the kind of person He wants you to be.

When I first came to know God, it was in a time of personal confusion and turmoil. I said, "God, if you are there, do something. Let me know." He did something. He let me know. He led a person into my life who explained how I could know Him. He will do the same for you, one way or another. God will not turn away anyone who turns to Him, and He has promised that any who seek Him honestly and diligently will find Him (see Jeremiah 29:13).

In summary, whatever you think about ultimate matters—how the universe and life came to be, or whether or not God exists—you believe by faith and not simply by unambiguous, overwhelming, public evidence. Even if you do not believe in God, you are still exercising faith. So why believe in God? Because He fully explains the existence of the universe, its complexity, purpose and design, and the uniqueness of humanity. Only God explains these and also offers Himself to be known by those who diligently seek Him.

SPEED BUMP!

Slow down to be sure you've gotten the main points of this section.

1. How does God explain the existence of the universe?
Every effect must have an adequate cause, and God is the only cause adequate for the existence of the universe.

2. How does God explain the order and purpose in the universe?
The order and purpose in the universe suggest an intelligent creator behind it.

3. How does God explain the uniqueness of humanity?
Humankind is a higher being than all other animals, and being created in the image of God explains why.

4. How does biblical evidence demand the existence of God?
The Bible concurs with our observations about life and the universe, and describes the God who made it.

FOR FURTHER STUDY

Scripture Passages

- Job 38:1–39:30
- Psalm 19:1–6
- Ecclesiastes 3:11
- Isaiah 40:12–17
- Isaiah 40:26
- Acts 14:17
- Romans 1:18–20

Read these passages and consider how they integrate with arguments for God's existence.

FAQ #5

 How Do We Define God?

 God is an infinite, eternal spirit, creator of the universe and sovereign over it.

While this definition is not complete, it is accurate as far as it goes. It would take a large book to define God fully, and even then it would be incomplete. But here we have a starting point. When we refer to the God of Christianity, our definition of God is not left up to our own discretion but must be determined from the pages of the Bible. Individual speculation has no more validation than a roll of the dice. The God we are talking about is the creator of the universe, the original being, the sovereign ruler of all that is, the sole judge of all that is true and false, right and wrong, good and bad. He is the One who communicated to humankind generally in nature and specifically through the words of the Bible.

The fourth question in the Westminster Shorter Catechism, a teaching curriculum used in many Presbyterian churches, is "What is God?" The answer is, "God is a Spirit, infinite, eternal, and unchangeable in His being, wisdom, power, holiness, justice, goodness and truth." This is a statement which the late theologian Charles Hodges described as "probably the best definition of God ever penned by man."

We must know God if we are to trust Him. We must trust Him if we are to obey

Why I Need to Know Who God Is

Today, there is no common understanding of who God is. Many people make up their own definition of who God is. We must be sure we are talking about the same God when we address the question, "Who is God?"

Him. We must obey Him if we are to have meaningful life on earth and eternal life in heaven. And we can only obey Him if we know who He is; that is, what His characteristics are, what He is like.

When discussing what God is like, it is helpful to divide His characteristics into two categories: those He shares with humanity (sometimes called his moral attributes, or his communicable attributes), and those He does not share with humanity (sometimes called his natural attributes, or his incommunicable attributes, which are unique to Him alone).

The characteristics that God shares with humanity are greatly diminished in people, but they are similar enough to allow a relationship to exist. An analogy may be seen in the relationship between people and pets. While a person's intelligence and emotional makeup are far superior to a dog's, the dog has enough intelligence and emotional capacity for both the owner and the dog to have an enjoyable and satisfying relationship.

God is infinite and sovereign over creation.

My wife and I used to have a large black standard poodle. The image that pops into your mind when I say that would be quickly dispelled if you were to have seen her. For example, we did not give her a "poodle cut." We cut her au naturel. Every hair on her body was about two inches long. She looked much like a black sheepdog. In many ways she was intelligent, but in some ways she seemed retarded. She never obeyed us, but she almost always agreed with us, so that we lived together rather harmoniously. She was so smart that there were certain words my wife and I could not say in conversation with one another, words like "ride," "food," "treat," "car," "vet," and others. If we said them, she flew into a whirling dervish of anticipation. If we spelled them, she became inquisitive. She was the most sanguine dog I have ever seen. Everywhere we went, she thought she was leading a parade. She would grab a stick or something, throw her head in the air and bounce along in front of us as though she had been given the key to the city. Our neighbors loved her, our friends loved her, and even our vet loved her. Everyone loved Sugar Bear. She had enough intelligence and emotional capacity to endear herself to us. It was a dark day indeed when she was killed by a large truck (she hated trucks). She was either too dumb or too smart to be broken of the dangerous habit of chasing trucks, and in the end it proved fatal.

I don't want to insult anyone by comparing him to a dog. I just want to make the point that living things do not have to be on an equal plane in order to have a meaningful relationship. We loved Sugar Bear, just as many of you love your pets, even though they are not on an equal plane with you.

Therein lies an analogy between mankind and God. We are not on an equal plane with God, but we share enough characteristics with Him that we can have a meaningful relationship with Him. Therefore, when addressing the question, "Who is God?", it is helpful to look at characteristics that God and humanity have in common which enable humanity and God to have a relationship.

FAQ #6

 What Characteristics Does God Share with Humanity?

 Among the characteristics which God shares with humanity are His holiness, love, justice, and goodness.

Holiness

The holiness of God is difficult to define. Most definitions are so technical that an average person gets lost in the words and cannot grasp or appreciate what is being said. I am going to try to simplify the concept, which requires caution because you run the risk of distorting the truth. To prevent that, though, I will not say everything that could be said about holiness. I will try not to say anything inaccurate. When a basic grasp is gained, more complex and complete explanations may be studied later.

In completely reduced form, holiness means "without sin." To say that God is holy is to say that He is without sin. Yet we must say more. Not only has God never sinned, He is incapable of sin. That is His character, His very nature. Anything that is like God is not sin. Anything that is not like God is sin. It is not that He conforms to some high standard. He is the standard. Holiness means, on one hand, a complete absence of moral evil, but on the other hand it implies moral perfection. All that is good is bound up in God's character. Anything that departs from God's character is evil.

God is holy.

Holiness is God's most clearly defining characteristic. We see two dramatic statements concerning the holiness of God in Scripture. One is in the book of the prophet Isaiah:

In the year of King Uzziah's death, I saw the Lord sitting on a throne, lofty and exalted, with the train of his robe filling the temple. Seraphim stood above Him, each having six wings; with two he covered his face, and with two he covered his feet, and with two he flew. And one called out to another and said, "Holy, Holy, Holy is the Lord of hosts, the whole earth is full of His glory." And the foundations of the thresholds trembled at the voice of him who called out, while the temple was filling with smoke.

Then I said, "Woe is me, for I am ruined!
Because I am a man of unclean lips,
And I live among a people of unclean lips;
For my eyes have seen the King, the Lord of
hosts."

Then one of the seraphim flew to me, with a burning coal in his hand which he had taken from the altar with tongs. And he touched my mouth with it and said, "Behold, this has touched your lips; and your iniquity is taken away and your sin is forgiven.

Then I heard the voice of the Lord, saying, " Whom shall I send,
and who will go for Us?" Then I said, "Here am I, send
me."(Isaiah 6:1–8, NASB)

From this passage, we learn why holiness is God's most defining
characteristic. This is a vision of the Lord in the temple. God is high
and lifted up. Smoke is filling the temple. The whole temple, which
was a solid, sturdy building, shook as the angel spoke. This was a terrifying scene. Try to imagine yourself in the picture. What would you
do? I would fall to the floor and try to crawl into the nearest crack!
It would scare the wits out of me.

Isaiah's reaction was "Woe is me!" Why? Because he knew he had

God's Characteristics
We Can "Catch"

God's personal characteristics fall into two categories: those which
humanity also possesses, and those which humanity does not possess. The first are often called moral attributes, or communicable
attributes (meaning they can be shared or passed on to others, as
in a communicable disease, like the measles). The second are
often called natural attributes, or incommunicable attributes
(meaning they cannot be shared or passed on to others, as in
incommunicable diseases, such as heart disease, which you cannot
"catch" by being around someone with heart disease). God's
moral attributes can be summarized:

- Holiness (God is morally pure, without sin).
- Love (God desires that which is best for others).
- Justice (God applies consequences to people's actions according
  to fixed standards).
- Goodness (God's will ultimately brings about that which is grati-
  fying, beneficial, and morally upright).

sin in his life (I am a man of unclean lips), and the One before him had no sin. He feared that he would die because he was in the presence of the Holy One.

This shows us another characteristic of holiness. Not only does it have no sin, it cannot tolerate sin. It cannot be in the presence of sin. It is untouched by sin and untouchable by sin. There is a great gulf between man and God created by sin. God is holy. We are not. That is, until God works in us. When Isaiah repented of his sin God forgave him, which is symbolized in the hot coal touching his lips. When Isaiah repented and had been forgiven, he was accepted into the presence of God. Furthermore, when God asked "Whom shall I send, and who will go for Us?", Isaiah did not then shrink back from God. His sense of forgiveness took away his fear of being in the presence of this terrifying being. As a result, when Isaiah volunteered, God did not shrink back from Isaiah. Holiness had made the sinner holy and full acceptance followed.

Yes, God is holy. His holiness is a consuming fire (Hebrews 12:29). There is no evil in holiness, and holiness will not tolerate the presence of evil. God, in the end, will therefore destroy all evil, all that is not holy. It is a cause for terror to those who have not been made holy by the work of forgiving grace through faith in Jesus Christ. To those who have, it removes the breach, and therefore the terror. The newly-made holy ones may call the eternal Holy One "Abba," a term of endearment most closely translated "Daddy" (Romans 8:15).

Would you like confirmation of this? Second Corinthians 5:17 says, "if anyone is in Christ, he is a new creation; the old things have passed away; behold, all things have become new." The "old" that has passed away is the old self. Ephesians 4:22 and 24 say, "Lay aside the old self…and put on the new self which in the likeness of God has been created in righteousness and holiness of the truth." Your new self has been re-created by God. And having been born again (John 3:3), your new self is holy, just as God is holy.

Of course, this "new self" is still housed in an unchanged body, in which the power of sin still dwells (Romans

7:18–19). But the day will come when your new spiritual self will be joined with a redeemed body, and you will serve the Lord unimpeded by sin (Romans 8:23). In that day, in the fullness of all it means to be a holy creature, you will have full fellowship with a holy God.

Love

When we think of the love of God, it is easy to misunderstand what it means. Love is probably the first positive characteristic which people connect with God, but it is misunderstood. We hear statements such as, "A loving God would never send anyone to hell." Or, "A loving God would not allow such suffering in the world." Statements like these compel us to go to the Bible, where we will see, for example, that though hell and suffering are real, neither means that God is not love.

God is love.

Most of us tend to attach a human level of love to God, an emotional, warm, and fuzzy kind of love, because that is our concept of a loving person. When we say, "She is such a loving person," we usually mean that she is warm, giving, and compassionate. God is these things, but He is other things too. All God's characteristics are integrated. He does not exercise one characteristic in isolation from his other characteristics.

There are three words in the original Greek New Testament that translated into English as the one word "love." This often causes some confusion.

- *Eros* is physical, sensual love. We get our word "erotic" from this Greek word. This is not what is meant when the Bible says God is love.
- *Philos* is emotional love, such as one might have for a mother, father, or close friend. We get our English words philanthropist (love of man) and Philadelphia (brotherly love) from this Greek word. This is not what is meant when the Bible says God is love.

■ *Agape* (pronounced uh-gop'-ay) means to exercise one's will for the good of another. We have no common English words for it. When the Bible says that God is love, it says that God is "agape." It is the commitment to do good for another person, regardless of whether it feels good or is commended by others.

The primary characteristic of agape is that it gives. We see in John 3:16, "For God so loved the world that He gave." In Ephesians 5:25, we read, "Husbands, love your wives, just as Christ also loved the church and gave Himself for her."

The agape which God gives to us is beyond comprehension. The price which God has paid to love humanity is unimaginable. I heard a story (I was told it was true) in which a little girl needed a blood transfusion. The only one who had blood compatible with hers was her younger brother. The young boy's mother and father asked him if he would be willing to give his blood to save his sister. He thought about it gravely for some time and then decided that he would. As he was lying in the hospital bed, donating a harmless pint of blood, he looked up to his parents and asked, "When do I die?" He thought he had to give all his blood and that it would kill him! Yet he was willing to do it anyway. That is a glimpse of the kind of love God has for us.

The most obvious sacrifice God made for us is that He sent His Son Jesus to die for the sins of the world. Jesus came to earth, took on the form of human flesh as Jesus of Nazareth, lived a life of dramatic suffering and rejection, which culminated in His being crucified, a particularly cruel form of capital punishment exercised by the Roman government. That would be bad enough, but many people were crucified. Jesus was not the only one. In addition to His life of rejection culminating in His crucifixion, Jesus, at the moment of His death, took on Himself all the sins of the world. Jesus "bore our sins in His own body on the tree"(1 Peter 2:24). The Crucifixion brought to Jesus an anguish which no human can experience or comprehend. Many theologians and Bible teachers agree that Jesus outsuffered any human who ever lived.

Many years ago, the U.S.S. Pueblo, a ship from the United States Navy, was hijacked by the North Korean military. The incident provoked deep tension worldwide, provoking a diplomatic and military standoff for several days. The eighty-two surviving crew members were thrown into a period of brutal captivity. For example, thirteen of the captured sailors were forced to sit in a rigid manner around a table. After several hours of strict immobility the door was flung open and a North Korean guard brutally beat the sailor in the first chair with the butt of his rifle. The next day, as each sailor sat at his assigned place, again the door was thrown open and the sailor in the first chair was violently beaten. On the third day it happened again to the same man. Knowing the man could not survive, another young sailor took his place. When the door was flung open the guard automatically beat the new victim senseless. For weeks, each day a different sailor stepped forward to sit in that horrible chair, knowing full well what would happen. At last the guards gave up in exasperation. They were unable to beat that kind of sacrificial love.

That is agape. God loves us with that kind of sacrificial love. Each of us was the person sitting in the designated chair doomed to punishment until Jesus traded places with us. Thus the Bible says, "But God demonstrates His own love toward us, in that while we were still sinners, Christ died for us" (Romans 5:8).

We may never have to die for someone, or take someone's beating, but 1 Corinthians 13:4–7 describes the kind of sacrificial love we must express to others, as we exemplify God's agape toward us:

Love suffers long and is kind; love does not envy; love does not parade itself, is not puffed up; does not behave rudely, does not seek its own, is not provoked, thinks no evil; does not rejoice in iniquity, but rejoices in the truth; bears all things, believes all things, hopes all things, endures all things.

As love is the motivating force of God, so, too, it must be for us.

Justice

We don't hear much about God's justice these days. It is not a popular concept because we live in a day when one of our highest values is personal independence. "I don't tell you how to live your life, so don't tell me how to live my life." It is considered highly impolite and unacceptable to stick one's nose into anyone else's business.

Nevertheless, justice is one of God's central characteristics. It can be defined as applying the consequences to a person's actions according to a fixed standard. The fixed standard says that if you do this, then such and such will follow. It is applied consistently to all people, without regard to favoritism or any other intervening thing.

God has said that "all have sinned and fall short of the glory of God" (Romans 3:23), and that the "wages of sin is death" (Romans 6:23). Therefore, God's justice requires that all die. However, His mercy is the characteristic that causes him to provide the way of escape when we deserve that judgment. We deserve to die, but God Himself, in Jesus, came to earth and died for us, so that if we believe in Him, and receive Him personally as our Savior, then God will count Jesus' death for ours, and we will receive God's gift of life. This way of escape from that judgment satisfies Him, and when we accept that way of escape, God is not unjust to save us.

God is merciful and just.

When we put God's justice and mercy together, it destroys the two most common misconceptions about God. The first misconception it destroys is that God is a celestial Santa Claus, winking and booming a cheery "Ho, ho, ho!" at our transgressions: "Humans will be humans." Nothing could be further from the truth. He has fixed standards, and violating those standards brings set consequences.

The other misconception it destroys is that God is a harsh, unfeeling judge who is watching from heaven, arms crossed, face in a scowl, just waiting for us to do something wrong so He can zap us with a lightning bolt. Instead of this, He loves us and is exceedingly merciful. He wants us to be able to avoid His judgment.

I heard a story, I don't know if it is true, about a young boy who disobeyed his father and was going to receive a spanking. He was taken to his bedroom and instructed to lean over the bed as his father wielded a wooden paddle. As the young boy closed his eyes and waited anxiously for the dreaded blows to fall, he heard the paddle strike but felt nothing. He heard it strike again and again but still did not feel anything. Finally he opened his eyes and saw his father striking himself on the thigh with the paddle as hard as he could. His father had taken the boy's punishment. God's justice and mercy are like that.

Goodness

To do good is one of the most respected things in the world. When one's character is known by the good he has done, that person becomes highly esteemed. We admire people who do good. When we see goodness, it touches us deeply. I remember many years ago reading a quote in a daily devotional magazine that touched me deeply, "We ought always be kind to others, for they may be walking life's road wounded." I thought of all the times I had been unkind to others, not because I meant to, but because I was walking life's road wounded. I resolved to be more kind. This helped me to see God's inherent goodness more clearly, and His intentions toward us.

It is such a wonderful thing that God is good. Think if He were not. There are, and have been, evil gods. These gods are either conjured up in people's minds and then foisted on others, or they may be demons. We have all seen images of evil-looking gods and faces of demons carved in wood or stone, and mythology is filled with gods. These are bad gods and false gods. It is a wonderful thing that the God of which we speak is good.

But what do we mean by good? "Good" is one of those words like "love"; it is hard to define, though we know it when we see it. It has been God's intention from the beginning of creation to do good. In Genesis 1, God repeatedly calls the things He has created "good" or "very good." He chose Israel out of all the nations of the world and promised to do good for her (Numbers 10:29). He gave Israel commandments "for your good" (Deuteronomy 10:13). David said in Psalm 119:68 that the Lord is good and that everything He does is good. Truly, the Lord is good (2 Chronicles 7:3).

In the New Testament, Jesus calls Himself the Good Shepherd (John 10:14). The apostle Paul wrote in Romans 8:28 that "all things work together for good to those who love God, to those who are the called according to His purpose." Romans 12:1–2 teaches us that God's will is good and perfect. In Philippians 1:6 we read that "He who has begun a good work in you will complete it until the day of Jesus Christ."

As part of His character, God extends that goodness to us. This means that everything God asks of us is for our good. In addition, He intends to extend to His children a gratifying, enjoyable, beneficial, and morally upright experience and relationship with Him.

Two extremes must be avoided in understanding the goodness of God. First, it must be understood that God is not out to please only Himself. What God is undertaking to do is desirable from the standpoint of His children. God is not an engineer or scientist fooling around with human toys for His own enjoyment. Instead, God is a caring Creator, as well as the Redeemer and Savior, and we can be sure that His goodness includes "goodness" from his children's point of view.

The second extreme to be avoided is that, when we say God intends to do good for His children, we think life will always be easy and pleasurable. Just as a surgeon must sometimes hurt in order to heal, so God sometimes allows pain into our lives, and then uses it for a good purpose. God delivers us through the pain inherent in a fallen world, but not always from it. Suffering is part of the Christian experience. But in the pain, and through the life of sin into which we are all born, God will work good in our lives, and in the end He will usher us into a life of unbroken bliss with Him as He does "good" for us forever.

God is good.

SPEED BUMP!

Slow down to be sure you've gotten the main points in this section.

1. How do we define God?
God is an infinite, eternal spirit, creator of the universe and sovereign over it.

2. What characteristics does God share with humanity?
Among the characteristics which God shares with humanity are His moral characteristics of holiness, love, justice, and goodness.

FOR FURTHER STUDY

Scripture Passages

- Luke 7:29; 18:2–7: God is just
- John 3:5–7; 4:23–24: God is spirit
- Romans 8:28; Romans 12:1–2; 3 John 11: God is good
- 1 John 4:7–19: God is love
- Revelation 4 & 5: God is holy

Read these passages and consider how they augment your understanding of who God is.

FAQ #7

 Does God Have a Beginning and an End?

 God is eternal, existing without a beginning or an end.

When I was about junior high age, I went through a time in which I did not go to sleep easily at night. I would lie awake as my mind wandered to imponderable subjects. I used to think a lot about infinity of distance. I used to imagine the infinite distance that I thought existed in the universe. If you went straight up for a million, billion, trillion, quadrillion miles into the universe and came to a brick wall, all you would have to do is crawl over the brick wall and keep going to realize that you had only begun. There was, and could be, I reasoned, no end to space. Or if space ended and something else was there, there could be no end to it. There could be no end to distance. Whenever you thought you were at the end of "distance," there was always something on the other side. My mind would reel at the impossibility, and yet necessity, of such a thought. Such thoughts would begin to unnerve me, even frighten me a little, and I would deliberately pull back mentally. I didn't understand why my thoughts frightened me, but the closer I came to feeling that I was grasping infinity of distance, the more frightened I got.

God **is eternal.**

I would also think about eternity of time. I had no difficulty starting with a fixed point in time, like my birthday, and going on forever. Time, like distance, could not end. But what I had great difficulty with was to go backward and realize that time could have no beginning. That really freaked me out. No end to time in the future I could handle, but no beginning—that was too much. I couldn't handle it. I would get frightened and pull back.

My mind was just as capable of understanding those matters then as it is now. But I realize now that, in a figurative sense, my finite mind was reaching out and touching the infinite mind of God, and I was not capable of mastering the moment. My reach exceeded my grasp. As if shot out of a cannon, I turned, yelping and crying as though I were being stung by a thousand bees.

Though I had never been instructed in theology, my mind was, instinctively, rubbing shoulders with one of the great characteristics of God: He has no end. That, I have no trouble with. But He has no beginning—it can't be. But it must be.

God is eternal. He never had a beginning, and he will never have an end (Psalm 90:2). It is a very reassuring thought to me. It makes me feel safe. The universe can make sense to me. He always has been, and He always will be, and I am safe, loved, and significant.

> The reason the mass of men fear God, and at bottom dislike Him, is because they rather distrust His heart, and fancy Him all brain, like a watch.
>
> *Herman Melville*

FAQ #8

 Does God Ever Change?

 God is immutable, He has never changed and will never change.

Another important characteristic of God is that He never changes (Hebrews 13:8). Theologians call this characteristic "immutability," which Webster defines simply as "unchanging." All change must be for the better or for the worse. If God is perfect, He could not change for the better. You cannot improve on perfection. And, if He is perfect, He cannot change for the worse for the same reason. If God ever changed, or ever could change, we could never be sure of anything.

God cannot change because His very nature is unchanging. Therefore, He can never be wiser, more holy, more just, more merciful, more truthful; nor less. Nor do His plans and purposes change. He is the same yesterday, today, and forever. The apostle James writes that God is "the Father of lights, with whom there is no variation or shadow of turning" (James 1:17). Malachi writes that "I am the Lord, I do not change" (Malachi 3:6).

God is immutable.

A contradiction seems to come when we read a passage such as Numbers 23:19, which says that God does not repent (change His mind), and a passage such as Exodus 32:14, which says that God changed His mind. However, it can be resolved fairly easily. It is precisely because God is unchanging in His moral character that evokes different responses from Him when people themselves change their minds. In Jeremiah 18:7–10, we read:

*The instant I speak concerning a nation and concerning a king-
dom, to pluck up, to pull down, and to destroy it, if that nation
against whom I have spoken turns from its evil, I will relent of
the disaster that I thought to bring upon it.*

So it is not inconsistent for God to change His mind and refrain
from judgment when a nation repents. His specific actions might
change, but His nature, character, and purposes do not.

FAQ #9

 Is God Everywhere?

 **God is omnipresent, He is everywhere
simultaneously.**

The next three characteristics form a well-known triad, each one
beginning with the syllable "omni," which means "unlimited." (If
you are omnivorous, it means you will eat anything.) The first
one is "omnipresence," meaning that God is everywhere
present simultaneously. In Psalm 139:7–10 we read,
"Where can I go from Your Spirit? Or where can I
flee from Your presence? If I ascend into heav-
en, You are there; if I make my bed in hell,
behold, You are there. If I take the wings
of the morning, and dwell in the uttermost
parts of the sea, even there Your hand shall lead
me, and Your right hand shall hold me."

God is omnipresent

There is nowhere we can go and not be in the presence
of God. As Paul Little has observed in his book *Know What You
Believe*, "He is not like a substance spread out in a thin layer all over

the earth—all of Him is in Chicago, in Calcutta, in Cairo, and in Caracas, at one and the same time."

Now there are some important implications to omnipresence. One is that omnipresence is not pantheism. Omnipresence states that God is everywhere. Pantheism states that everything is God, or a part of God. If you were sitting in a tree, omnipresence says that God is present with you. Pantheism states that the tree is God. The God of the Bible, however, is separate and distinct from His creation, though He is present with it.

Second, omnipresence means that you cannot sin without sinning in the presence of God. If you are tempted to tell a little white lie to someone you don't know, God is present. If you are tempted to commit a sexual sin with another person, God is there. If you are tempted to falsify your income tax report in the privacy of your own study, God is there. You cannot sin without sinning in the presence of God.

Third, omnipresence means that God is always with you. You are not alone. Loneliness is one of the greatest emotional problems of the day. Billy Graham has stated that when he preaches on loneliness, he gets a greater response than on any other topic. Because God is omnipresent, the person who is alone or lonely can take comfort from that. God is there. Many reports of prisoners of war and hostages, who have spent many years isolated, have reported that knowing that God was present sustained their faith.

FAQ #10

 Does God Know Everything?

 God is omniscient, He knows all things, both actual and possible.

I have flown quite a bit in the last twenty years. I like to get to the airport with five minutes to spare. My idea of a perfect arrival is to be let off at the curb, check my luggage, walk briskly to the gate just as they are ready to close the door on the plane. This drives many people crazy. My mother-in-law is a careful flyer. She likes to arrive at least one hour ahead of time, to make sure that if you have a flat tire on the way you will still make your flight. Hers is the more prudent way, but I couldn't do it if my life depended on it. And it has been my observation that early arrivers miss as many planes as late arrivers. I have missed only one plane because of a purely late arrival. I have missed another plane because the airport people mover system broke down while I was in it. I missed another plane because I was reading the sports section of the San Francisco newspaper in a remote section of the airport while I had a two-hour layover. Dumb. Expensive.

My most mind-boggling experience came several years ago when I was living in Austin, Texas. I was flying to Atlanta through Dallas. My American Airlines flight left Austin for Dallas at 6:30 A.M., and left Dallas for Atlanta at 8:30 A.M. In Austin, I walked in a sleepy blur to the gate that said Dallas, 6:30 A.M. The flight attendant looked at my boarding pass and invited me to board. I settled in for what I knew would be at least thirty more minutes of sleep. We landed, and as I got off of the plane the red-jacketed man meeting the flight asked me if I had a connecting flight. I said I did, flight 1242.

God

is omniscient

"Sir, we have no flight 1242," the man said.

"Of course you do," I said, and showed him my ticket.

"Sir, that's an American Airlines ticket."

I blinked hard. "Who are you?" I asked thickly.

"Delta," he replied.

I stared at him blankly. On the outside I was the picture of sober control and decorum, but inside my mind was screaming, "Delta? How in the world could you be Delta? I flew American! Where am I? Who am I? What has happened?" My mind raced for some snatch of meaning. I felt as though I were in the Twilight Zone. Eventually I was able to speak.

"How did I get here?"

"Sir, I have no idea."

"Where is this?"

"Dallas, sir."

Dallas. At least I'm at the right airport. N-No need to p-panic. All I have to do is take the people mover to the American terminal, which I have enough time to do, and take my flight to Atlanta. Everything is okay. Everything is okay. Everything is okay.

I got on my American Airlines flight to Atlanta, but for the life of me I have a hard time figuring out what happened. The best I can guess is that both American Airlines and Delta had flights leaving Austin for Dallas at 6:30 that morning, and that the gates were right next to each other. By the time I arrived, everyone else was on board, they were in a hurry, and the flight attendant did not check my boarding pass carefully enough. In the providence of God, the plane was going to Dallas and not Singapore!

I have often thought of that incident. I was one person in one place at one point in time, in a circumstance in which there are many safeguards built in, and still, something went wrong. Can you imagine what the world would be like if God did not know everything? We'd all be in Singapore!

The second "omni" characteristic of God is His "omniscience," which means that God knows everything, both actual and possible. Psalm 139:4 reads, "For there is not a word on my tongue, but behold, O LORD, You know it altogether." When we say God knows everything, we mean that He knows all things, both actual and possible. In Matthew 11:21, Jesus said, "If the mighty works which were done in you had been done in Tyre and Sidon, they would have repented long ago in sackcloth and ashes."

God knows everything about everything. "The very hairs of your head are all numbered," Jesus said (Luke 12:7). Not even one sparrow is forgotten by God (Luke 12:6). God even knows our thoughts and intents (Heb. 4:12).

The implications of God's omniscience are similar to the implications for His omnipresence. First, it is a comfort to His children. No piece of information that God needs to keep his children safe will escape His notice. No knowledge needed to correct a mishap or solve a problem is missing. Do you hurt? God knows. Are you lonely? God knows. Are you confused? God knows. Do you have need? God knows. And even though He knows our every thought, He still loves us. The apostle Paul wrote, God "demonstrates His own love toward us, in that while we were still sinners, Christ died for us" (Romans 5:8). Every sin we would ever commit was in the future when Christ died for us, and yet He died for us anyway. Take heart. God knows, and He loves us anyway.

On the other side of the ledger, there is no hoodwinking God. There is no wool to be pulled over His eyes. Jeremiah wrote, "I, the LORD, search the heart, I test the mind, even to give every man according to his ways, according to the fruit of his doings" (Jeremiah 17:10). Here is the futility of trying to hide sin from God. We've got the spotlights at Carnegie Hall trained on us. Hypocrisy is ludicrous. Sneaking is ridiculous. Are you trying to put one over on God? Think again. Nothing we can think or do will escape His attention.

The philosopher Seneca once wrote, "I will govern my life and thoughts as if the whole world were to see the one and read the other, for what does it signify to make anything a secret to my neighbor, when to God, who is the searcher of our hearts, all our privacies are open?"

FAQ #11

 Can God Do Anything He Wants?

 God is omnipotent, He can do whatever He chooses."

The final "omni" characteristic of God is His power. Omnipotence means that God can do anything He chooses. Job 42:2 reads, "I know that You can do everything, and that no purpose of Yours can be withheld from You." He put the galaxies in place. He breathed life into a lump of clay and created man.

It is by looking at nature, and specifically "space," that we get some feel for God's omnipotence. We used to think that the universe was simply our Milky Way Galaxy. Today we know that galaxies are as common as blades of grass in a meadow. They number perhaps a hundred billion.

God is omnipotent.

How does one comprehend the incredible size of this galaxy-filled universe? For such awesome distances, scientists and astronomers think in terms of time, and they use the telescope as a time machine. They measure space by a unit called the light-year, the distance light travels in one year at the rate of 186,282 miles per second—about six trillion miles ("The Incredible Universe" p. 589).

We could look at the incredible temperatures generated with our sun, or we could marvel at the way our body knows how to respond to infection. Our God created these systems. He can do anything He chooses. He is able to provide for our every need.

THINKING BACK

"Knowing God" begins with believing the truth about Him. If we doubt one of these characteristics, we erode our basis for knowing God. We begin by accepting that these things are true of God. He is loving. He is just. He is merciful. He is all powerful. He is all knowing. He is present everywhere. He has no beginning or end. Accepting the truth of what we know about God is

God's "Omni" Attributes

omni = unlimited

omnipresent = unlimited presence. God is everywhere simultaneously.

omniscient (knowledge) = unlimited knowledge. God knows all things both actual and possible.

omnipotent (power) = unlimited power. God is able to do whatever He chooses.

the first step in knowing Him intimately. We learn to know God intimately as we come to see Him act consistently and predictably with these characteristics.

If we truly believed these things about God, it would radically change our attitude and behavior toward Him. We are warmed by these thoughts as we read about them or hear them preached on Sunday morning, but let Monday morning come and there is a distinct shift in our thinking. We find a memo in our box that someone younger, with less seniority in the company, has just been promoted ahead of us. We are now going to be working for that young little jerk who isn't even dry behind the ears. Our stomach is pumped full of acid, our bloodstream is injected with bile, and our heart starts pounding from adrenaline. We are angry and we are hurt. We're disappointed and frankly, a little scared. So where is God? Where is the steady direction of His will toward my welfare? That nice little homily suddenly seems cold, distant, and unrelated to the real world. Merciful, is He?

The Importance of God Being...

1. If God is not eternal, it means He is not the final answer for the existence of the universe. There is something greater than God.
2. If God is not unchangeable, then He might tell us one thing and do another.
3. If God is not omnipresent, then we might end up in trouble, and God would not be there to help.
4. If God is not omniscient, then He might be ignorant of something terribly important.
5. If God is not omnipotent, then He might want to do something we need but not be able to. God may be loving, kind, and merciful, as we saw in the last chapter but not be able to do anything about it. These unique characteristics are crucial if God is to be God.

Does He know about the little twerp I'm going to have to work for now? Omniscient? Did He know this was coming? Omnipotent? Was He able to do anything about it? Love? Does He care about this situation?

You see, the problem isn't that we have trouble understanding the attributes of God. It is that we have trouble reconciling them with the real world, with our experience and observation. If God is good, what happened to my job, my marriage, my kids? What is happening to my health, my finances, my friends?

We are to serve God, not be served.

Sure, we can understand the concepts of love, mercy, omnipotence and omniscience. They just don't seem to be present in the world we live in. So how do we put these characteristics into our life Monday morning? What does God have to say about that?

If the Holy Spirit were able to speak directly to you, I think He might say something like:

For what credit is it if, when you are beaten for your faults, you take it patiently? But when you do good and suffer, if you take it patiently, this is commendable before God. For to this you were called, because Christ also suffered for us, leaving us an example, that you should follow His steps; who committed no sin, nor was deceit found in His mouth; who, when He was reviled, did not revile in return; while He suffered, He did not threaten, but committed Himself to Him who judges righteously (1 Peter 2:20–23).

The sufferings of this present time are not worthy to be compared with the glory which shall be revealed in us (Romans 8:18).

Therefore we do not lose heart, even though our outward man is perishing, yet the inward man is being renewed day by day. For our light affliction, which is but for a moment, is working for us a far more exceeding and eternal weight of glory, while we do not look at the things which are seen, but at the

things which are not seen. For the things which are seen are
temporary, but the things which are not seen are eternal (2
Corinthians 4:17–18).

In other words, "I promised you a rose garden in the next life,
and enough grace for the thorns in this life. I promised you that, if
you would dedicate your life to me totally, and live for my values, I
would use you significantly in ministry to others and would fill your
life with peace, love and joy. The problem is that you are living for
this world, and you feel that I am here to make your life comfortable
in this world, and I have failed you if I don't give you the things you
want in this world. You have things backward. You are to serve Me.
I am not to serve you."

God loves us. Always. He always directs His purposes for our welfare. He never varies from that. He is merciful. He is omnipotent. He
is omniscient. He is omnipresent. It is just that, from time to time, we
forget where we are. We are visitors in this world. We are not home
yet.

You will be treated poorly in this life. You will not get the reward
that is due you. That doesn't change one thing about who God is. It
only means that you are not home yet. So, "be steadfast, immovable,
always abounding in the work of the Lord, knowing that your labor is
not in vain in the Lord" (1 Corinthians 15:58).

SPEED BUMP!

**Slow down to be sure you've gotten the main points
of this section.**

1. Does God have a beginning and an end?
God is eternal, existing without a beginning or an end.

2. Does God ever change?
God is immutable, He has never changed and will never change.

3. Is God everywhere?
God is omnipresent, He is everywhere simultaneously.

4. Does God know everything?

God is omniscient, He knows all things, both actual and possible.

5. Can God do anything He wants?

God is omnipotent, He can do whatever He chooses.

FOR FURTHER STUDY

Scriptures Passages

- Psalm 90:2; Genesis 21:33: God is eternal
- Hebrews 13:8; James 1:17: God is immutable
- Jeremiah 23:24; Psalm 139:7–10: God is omnipresent
- Matthew 11:21; Psalm 139:2; John 2:25: God is omniscient
- Job 42:2; Psalm 135:5–6: God is omnipotent

Read these passages and consider how they expand your understanding of God.

FAQ #12

 How Many Gods Does the Bible Teach There Are?

 The Bible teaches that there is only one God.

That there is only one God is a teaching heavily emphasized in the Old Testament. The message of God's unity was elevated in a time and place when many gods were recognized by those who were not Jews. For the most part, these gods were abominable deities, promoting immorality, self-indulgence, and profound cruelty as a basis for appeasement. There were three gods who had particularly high profiles, and who were especially odious to the true God, Jehovah.

Baal means "master." He was the "sun god," the most important god worshiped by the Canaanites (those who lived in the Promised Land before and after the Israelites took up residence there after their captivity in Egypt). He was the god of fertility, worshiped extensively in western Asia from Babylonia to Egypt. In the Old Testament his worship rivaled that of Jehovah and seems to have reached its height in Israel during the days of King Ahab and Jezebel (1 Kings 16–22). People who followed this god engaged in drunken sexual orgies as a way of worshiping him and invoking his blessing on their personal fertility. Altars were built in high places as centers for Baal worship, which was accompanied not only by drunken orgies but at times by the live sacrifice of children.

Ashtaroth was a Phoenician goddess similar to Baal, except that Baal was male. They were closely associated, and altars to Baal often accompanied an idol of Ashtaroth, suggesting that she was Baal's female partner.

Third was Molech, a particularly foul god of the Ammonites whose primary form of worship involved the burning of live children to him. These gods were so evil, it is not hard to see why Paul said that the "other gods" people worshiped were actually demons (1 Corinthians 10:20).

God is one.

The Old Testament emphasized that there was only one true God, and that He alone was to be worshiped. Thus God issued the first of His Ten Commandments: "You shall have no other gods before Me" (Exodus 20:3). Forty years later, by the inspiration of God, Moses declared, "Hear, O Israel: The LORD our God, the LORD is one! You shall love the LORD your God with all your heart, with all your soul, and with all your strength" (Deuteronomy 6:4–5).

The truth is affirmed in the New Testament. "We know that an idol is nothing in the world, and that there is no other God but one" (1 Corinthians 8:4). "[There is] one God and Father of all, who is above all, and through all, and in you all" (Ephesians 4:6). "You believe that there is one God. You do well" (James 2:19).

Both the Old and the New Testaments, therefore, affirm that there is only one true God.

FAQ #13

 Who Are Jesus and the Holy Spirit?

 In addition to God the Father, Jesus and the Holy Spirit are also called God in the Bible.

As we said, nowhere does the Bible use the term "Trinity." We get the idea from what the Bible says about the Father, Jesus, and the Holy Spirit.

First, we reiterate what is rarely debated, that the Father is God. The apostle John, recording the words of Jesus, says, "Do not labor for the food which perishes, but for the food which endures to everlasting life, which the Son of Man will give you, because God the Father has set His seal on Him" (John 6:27). Peter supports this when he mentions "God the Father" in 1 Peter 1:2. Few have difficulty with that.

But Jesus is also recognized as God in the New Testament. Jesus appeared to some of His disciples after His crucifixion and resurrection. However, Thomas (forever dubbed "Doubting Thomas" for his skeptical attitude) questioned the reality of their report. He stoutly declared that he would not believe unless he was able to put his fingers into Jesus' wounds. Strong words. I don't think he ever thought he would have to eat them. In a magnanimous gesture of accommodation, Jesus appeared to Thomas and said, "Reach your finger here, and look at My hands; and reach your hand here, and put it into My side. Do not be unbelieving, but believing." Thomas then answered Jesus with, "My Lord and my God!" (John 20:27–28). What a gracious act of kindness for

> Tell me how it is that in this room there are three candles and but one light, and I will explain to you the [Trinity].
>
> *John Wesley*

Jesus to have done that. For the sake of one man who expressed not cynicism, but honest reservation, Jesus went the extra mile to win him over. He does that with anyone who expresses honest questions, in a desire, not to reject the truth, but to know it.

Apart from clear testimony as to who He was, Jesus did and said things that can be interpreted only as divine. In a remarkable passage in Mark 2:1–12, Jesus was teaching in a home so crowded that no one else could get in. As a result, the friends of a paralytic man began tearing off the roof of the house to let him down by Jesus to be healed. It wasn't difficult to spot the faith behind their dramatic actions. Jesus said to the paralytic man, "My son, your sins are forgiven." With this, the religious leaders went ballistic. Heads jerked. Veins popped. Jaws went slack. What had they heard? This was blasphemy! No one can forgive sins but God! Knowing their thoughts, Jesus said, "Which is easier, to say to the paralytic, 'Your sins are forgiven you,' or to say 'Arise, take up your bed and walk'?"

God is tri-unity, three "persons" in one Being.

The answer is, of course, it is easier to say "Your sins are forgiven you." Who is going to prove you wrong for such an unobservable phenomenon? So to prove that He acted with God's full authority, Jesus said, "Arise, take up your bed and walk." The point Jesus was making was, if He could heal a man of paralysis it would indicate that He could forgive sin, which would imply that He was God.

Jesus' words also betrayed that He was God. In John 8, Jesus was debating religious leaders who were looking for reasons to reject Him. They were arguing about whether Jesus was old enough to have seen Abraham, the father of all Jews who had lived two thousand years earlier. When Jesus said to them, "Most assuredly, I say to you, before Abraham was, I AM," the Jews picked up stones to throw at Him.

Why did they do that? Wasn't that an overreaction? Jesus was only off on His chronology by a couple of thousand years. Is that any reason to stone a man? The reason they tried to stone Him was because God's name, revealed to Moses in Exodus 3:14 and revered by devout Jews in Jesus' day, is "I AM." When Jesus, therefore, said, "I AM," the Jews knew He was claiming to be God. And to them, this was blasphemy. The penalty for blaspheming God was death by stoning. This conflict concerned no little chronological computing error. Jesus' identifying Himself as I AM drew a line in the sand, and the Jews either had to accept Jesus or reject Him. They rejected Him (John 8:58–59).

A similar event occurred in John 10:30–33, where Jesus said, "I and My Father are one." When the Jews took up stones to stone Him, Jesus asked, "For which of [my good] works do you stone me?" And the Jews replied, "For a good work we do not stone You, but for blasphemy, and because You, being a man, make Yourself God."

Make no mistake. The Jews understood the significance of Jesus' deeds and words. They knew He was claiming to be God.

Finally, we come to the Holy Spirit. The Bible also presents Him, unambiguously, as God. Early on in the Acts of the Apostles, many of the first Christians in Jerusalem were living in a communal situation, probably because of the persecution of Christians which sprang up with

Gods of Ancient Israel's Neighbors

Three popular false gods widely worshiped in the Middle East during Old Testament times were:

1. Baal, the Canaanite sun god of fertility. Canaan corresponds with modern-day Israel. Canaanites lived there until Israel became a nation. Some Canaanite people lived there even after that and kept alive the dreadful worship of Baal.

2. Ashtaroth, the Phoenician goddess of fertility, the female partner of Baal. Phoenicia was a country just north of Israel, near modern-day Lebanon.

3. Molech, the national god of the Ammonites who demanded child sacrifice. Ammon generally corresponds with modern-day Jordan.

the crucifixion of Jesus. Also, the newness of what was happening, all the excitement, miracles, and explosive growth created an environment which made people want to stay together for the experience of it all. Many Jews who were there actually lived elsewhere, had come to Jerusalem for the Passover, and had not yet gone back home.

To survive, many people who had possessions sold them, and brought the money to the apostles to use for the needs of the whole group. A man named Joseph sold some property and brought the money from the sale and laid it at the apostles' feet.

Perhaps this seemed like an extraordinary gesture of generosity which made Joseph look very spiritual in the eyes of the new Christian community. In this context, a husband and wife named Ananias and Sapphira sold some real estate which they owned, kept some of the money for themselves, and brought the rest to the apostles. They must have made some kind of a statement or pretense when they gave the money, which led the people to believe that they had given all the money from the sale of the property. Either God or someone else let Peter know that they had not given all the money from the sale, and they misrepresented the facts. Peter called them on it. Paraphrasing, he said, "Ananias, why has Satan filled your heart to lie to the Holy Spirit, and to keep back some of the price of the land? No one forced you to sell the property, did they? And after you sold it, no one forced you to give even a thin dime to us. Yet, you have made it appear as though you gave all the money." Then he said, "You have not lied to men, but to God." In this passage, Peter equated lying to the Holy Spirit as lying to God. Also, the Holy Spirit has the same attributes as God, such as omniscience (1 Corinthians 2:10) and omnipresence (Psalm 139:7). He also existed before the creation of the world and participated in the creation (Genesis 1:2), along with God the Father and Jesus (Colossians 1:15–16).

And the Father, Son, and Holy Spirit are linked together in several key New Testament passages. In 2 Corinthians 13:13–14, Paul writes a benediction which includes all three: "The grace of the Lord Jesus Christ, and the love of God, and the communion of the Holy Spirit be with you all." If Jesus and the Holy Spirit were not God,

The Bible presents the Holy Spirit as God.

Paul would be presumptuous, indeed, to link them as equal with the Father. And there is the Trinitarian prayer for grace and peace from the Father, the Spirit, and Jesus Christ in Revelation 1:4–5. In the Trinitarian benediction, we see the Father mentioned first, the Son second, and the Spirit third. In the Revelation passage, we see the Father first, the Spirit second, and the Son third. This capacity to alter the order of persons reinforces their equality in the minds of the inspired writers of Scripture.

Jesus spoke and acted as God.

In Matthew 28:19, Jesus instructs the disciples to go and make disciples of all the nations, "baptizing them in the name [not names!] of the Father and of the Son and of the Holy Spirit." "These three persons are the one God to whom Christians commit themselves" (J. I. Packer, *Concise Theology*, p. 41).

And we also find the Trinity present at Jesus' baptism. Jesus is in the water, God the Father speaks from heaven, and the Holy Spirit descends on Jesus in the visible form of a dove (Mark 1:9–11).

Again, the Bible never uses the word "Trinity" or says that "God is three and yet one." However, Trinitarian faith and thinking are found throughout the Bible, and in that sense "Trinity" is sound doctrine.

FAQ #14

 Can the Doctrine of the Trinity Be Fully Explained?

 Attempts to explain the doctrine of the Trinity fully fall short, as do all attempts to explain God fully. The statements of Scripture that form this doctrine must be taken by faith at face value.

How do you reconcile the fact that the Old Testament seems very clear that God is one, supported by key passages in the New

Testament, and yet, in the New Testament, we see the Son and the Spirit being presented as having the same attributes as the Father and linked with the Father in apparent equality in two key passages?

The doctrine of the Trinity did not come first and the passages second. The passages came first, and the doctrine of the Trinity came as the best effort of devout, cautious, and thoughtful believers to harmonize the passages. I confess, I see no other solution to the passages than the historical doctrine of the Trinity.

An attempt to explain only the oneness destroys the threeness, and an attempt to explain only the threeness destroys the oneness. So what do we do? We have three choices. One, we can start whacking away at our Bibles, setting ourselves up as the judge as to what is acceptable and unacceptable in the Bible. Or, like the White Queen, we can believe impossible things. We can say, God is full of nonsense, but I believe it anyway. Or, we can admit that while we cannot fully understand it, it makes sense to God and will make sense to us when we stand before God. For now we choose to believe it even though it transcends our understanding.

The first option is mischievous because if you don't believe the

Distorted Views of God

Two prominent ancient views about God deny the Trinity and were considered and then rejected by early Christians as false (as heresies).

1. Arianism, propounded by a Greek theologian named Arius in the 4th century A.D., holds that there is only one God, Jehovah, denying that Jesus and the Holy Spirit are God.

2. Sabellianism, propounded by Sabellius, also agrees that there is only one God, but maintains that He is only one person who appears in three different manifestations (Father, Son, Holy Spirit), like an actor changing costumes. It thus denies that Christ and the Holy Spirit are distinct persons within the one Being of God.

entire Bible, where do you stop believing? With the Trinity? With the virgin birth of Christ? With a literal, bodily resurrection? Where do you stop? Deciding you are the judge over the Bible is like scooting off the top of an Olympic ski jump. There is no place to stop. Who knows enough to tinker with the Word of God? Because the Bible is God's book, I would rather place my confidence in it completely than I would my own judgment, or anyone else's. Denominations and parachurch organizations that started out selecting what they would believe and not believe in the Bible end up believing almost nothing of it.

Choosing the second option is to give ourselves over to nonsense. People who do this end up with a meaningless Bible.

The third option makes sense. Physicist Stephen Hawking, who is terribly disabled, lives in a wheelchair, and can barely communicate, has written a book entitled *A Brief History of Time.* He is considered by some to be the greatest scientific mind since Albert Einstein. His book was on the *New York Times* bestseller list for an impressive length of time for a book of that kind. But few people really understood it, requiring a second book to be written explaining the first one. If Stephen Hawking says things that go over our heads, is it any wonder that God says things that go over our heads?

If you start whacking out parts of the Bible, or chuck the Bible altogether because there are things in it you cannot understand, you solve one problem: You don't have to explain the Trinity and other hard things. But for every problem you solve, you create a hundred more.

There are really only two errors you can fall into regarding the Trinity. You can emphasize oneness to the detriment of threeness, or you can emphasize threeness to the detriment of oneness. Both of these errors have been made for the last two thousand years.

Arius, who lived in the early fourth century A.D. was a priest in North Africa who held the deity of the Father so highly that he denied that Jesus Christ and the Holy Spirit were also God, in every way equal to the Father. His was the first major ancient heresy regarding the doctrine of God. A modern heresy similar to it is unitarianism (The Unitarian Church), which likewise denies that Jesus Christ is God. Jehovah's Witnesses regard Arius as a forerunner of C. T. Russell, the founder of the sect. Arianism also has similarities with strict Mormonism, which claims that Jesus was created and not eternally divine.

Another heresy denies the eternal Trinity in favor of a God of one eternal person who merely shows Himself on different occasions as Father, Son, and Spirit. Sabellius, who lived around A.D. 250, was the first to champion this view called "modalism." Sabellius insisted that the one God appeared in three successive modes, first as Father, then as Son, and finally as the Holy Spirit. With the Arians, modalists maintain the unity of God; however, unlike the Arians, modalists also emphasize that Jesus Christ is fully God. Despite its commendable emphasis both on God's unity and on Jesus Christ's identity as God, modalism is flawed because it denies that the Father, the Son, and the Holy Spirit are distinct personally and eternally. Modalism tells us that God only appears in three different roles, leaving us unsure of who God really is behind or apart from these roles, or modes of manifestation. In contrast, the doctrine of the Trinity tells us that God is Father, Son, and Holy Spirit eternally.

The doctrine of the Trinity thus assures us that God's love toward us is nothing less than the same love that flows perfectly and eternally between the Father, the Son, and the Holy Spirit. But by denying these personal and eternal distinctions within the being of God, modalism (taught today by "oneness" Pentecostals) undermines our assurance of God's love for us and blurs the knowledge of God we enjoy through the clarity of the revealed doctrine of the Trinity.

Apart from these denials of the Trinity, one distortion of the Trinity remains a constant danger wherever the doctrine is not taught accurately. That danger is tritheism, a distortion of the Trinity that sees Father, Son, and Holy Spirit not as persons within the one Being of God, but instead as three distinct Gods. In this case, the threeness of God is not sufficiently integrated with His oneness. Tritheism is nowhere intentionally taught among Christians. Where it appears, it is the unfortunate result of inaccurate and careless teaching that allows some not to believe what the Bible from Genesis to Revelation consistently emphasizes: God is one.

THINKING BACK

In summary, then, we see that the doctrine of the Trinity is a vital doctrine. You cannot remain true to the teachings of the Scripture and hold to another position. You must whack something out of your Bible or add something to it. Consequently, we must give equal attention, value, and honor to each member of the Trinity. All non-Trinitarian teachings fall short of Scripture.

All too often, we in the West with our smug self-assurance demand that God be understandable and reasonable. As spiritual "ugly Americans" we look down on God and insist that He conform to our expectations. But let me ask, how simple would the Bible have to be in order for everyone to understand everything about it? Should a person with an I.Q. of 150 be able to understand everything about it? How about a person with an I.Q. of 110? What about 85? Should a child of ten be able to understand it all? How about a child of two? Should everyone be able to understand everything about the Bible, or only some people? Surely you are able to understand things now that you were not able to understand ten years ago.

It ought not to bother us if there are things we don't understand. I would be a little frightened if I understood everything about God. I would fear that He would be too simple to be able to solve all the problems. If I don't understand all the problems, why should I expect to understand all the solutions, or the Solution-giver? Let us decide to take God as He reveals Himself to us, and approach Him and His Word in humility and obedience.

We have finite minds. We will never be able to fully comprehend an infinite mind, or the Book that came out of it. The doctrine of the Trinity is a difficult doctrine; yet without committing intellectual suicide we can embrace it, realizing that the day will come when we shall know and understand more fully the God we worship. Sometimes, we have to see in order to believe. Other times, we must believe in order to see.

SPEED BUMP!

Slow down to be sure you've gotten the main points of this section.

1. **How many Gods does the Bible teach there are?**
The Bible teaches that there is only one God.

2. **Who are Jesus and the Holy Spirit?**
In addition to God the Father, Jesus and the Holy Spirit are also called God in the Bible.

3. **Can the doctrine of the Trinity be fully explained?**
Attempts to explain the doctrine of the Trinity fully fall short, as do all attempts to explain God fully. The statements of Scripture that form this doctrine must be taken by faith at face value.

FOR FURTHER STUDY

Scripture Passages

- ■ Deuteronomy 6:4
- ■ Matthew 3:17–17
- ■ Matthew 28:19
- ■ 2 Corinthians 13:14
- ■ 1 Peter 1:2

Read these passages and consider how they augment your understanding of the Trinity.

FAQ #15

 Who Is God the Father?

 The Father is God, the first member of the Trinity.

The Father of Us All, Including Jesus

God is a Spirit, but He is also our Father and all that that name implies. In Ephesians 1:2, we read, "Grace to you and peace from God our Father and the Lord Jesus Christ." In the next verse, we see that He is also the Father of Jesus: "Blessed be the God and Father of our Lord Jesus Christ."

Imagine in your mind's eye, as we did with Casper ten Boom, the finest earthly father you can imagine. God the Father is like that man, only more so. The Father is more loving, more caring, more wise, more knowledgeable, more zealous to provide for and protect, and more capable of fathering than any earthly father could be. We read in Hebrews 12:9–10 that

We had earthly fathers to discipline us, and we respected them; shall we not much rather be subject to the Father of spirits and live? For they disciplined us for a short time as seemed best to them, but He disciplines us for our good, that we may share His holiness (NASB).

Earthly fathers discipline imperfectly, but God the Father perfectly. It is no accident that our heavenly Father chose to be called by the same word as our earthly fathers. In our day, some people have had bad fathers, and that is unfortunate. But some of us have had good fathers, and it helps us imagine what God the Father is like. Even those who have had bad fathers have seen and wished for good fathers, enough to have some concept of the goodness of God the Father.

In God the Father exists the perfection of the Godhead, so we know that He is loving, compassionate, just, holy, merciful, righteous, all-knowing, all-powerful, everywhere present, unchanging, and timeless.

The **Father is perfect** **love.**

The Head of the Trinity

As the Father, He is the head of the Trinity. First Corinthians 11:3 says, "Christ is the head of man, and the man is the head of a woman, and God is the head of Christ." In other words, the Father is the final authority in the Trinity. To understand this authority, we must understand the biblical idea of authority and submission. The core concept is mutual submission, with each person submitting to one another.

While mutual submission is the spirit every Christian is to have toward others, there are, nevertheless, roles that Christians are to play toward others, even while having that spirit. For example, the instruction to "be subject to one another" in Ephesians 5 is followed by a description of three sets of relationships: husband/wife, parent/child, and master/slave. Paul describes how a husband is to submit to his wife and how his wife is to submit to her husband; how the parents are to submit to their children and how their children are to submit to their parents; how a master is to submit to his slave, and how the slave is to submit to his master.

The principle is laid down very clearly: In each relationship, the one in authority is to be submissive to the needs of the one under him, and the one under authority is to be submissive to the authority of the one over

An almost perfect relationship with his father was the earthly root of all [George McDonald's] wisdom. From his own father, he said, he first learned that Fatherhood must be at the core of the universe. He was thus prepared in an unusual way to teach that religion in which the relation of the Father and the Son is of all relations the most central.

C. S. Lewis

him. If this relationship exists, it results in peace, love, and harmony.

Now the next question is, "Why did God give us those instructions?" I believe the answer is that He has created humanity to thrive under the same principles which operate within Trinity. The Father is the authority in the Trinity. Jesus is submissive to that authority. The Holy Spirit serves both the Father and the Son. Peace, love, and joy are the primary characteristics of that relationship. If we want peace, love, and joy, we must function the same way.

Divine authority submits to the needs of those under authority.

The key to all significant relationships is the servant heart. It is being subject to one another; caring for another more than you care for yourself; putting someone else first. When we don't do this, relationships wither and die. Thus, when it comes to the success of the significant relationships in our lives, mutual submission is the secret. Throughout the Bible, whenever authority is given to anyone, that authority is to be used for the good of the one under authority, whether it is government to citizens, elders to congregation, husbands to wives, parents to children, or masters to slaves. God gives no one authority to do mischief.

Who is God the Father? He is the first person in the Trinity who is in authority in the Trinity and in all creation. He is our Heavenly Father, and, as our Father, is dedicated to doing good to us forever.

FAQ #16

 What Does God the Father Do?

 God the Father initiates in His relationship within the Trinity, and He provides for and protects His children.

While all three members of the Trinity are equal in worth, they do not all have the same role. God the Father does things that the Son does not do. The Son does things that the Spirit does not do. Their roles are distinct, even while enjoying equality in a spirit of mutual submission. The distinct roles of the Father are related to His position as the One in authority in the Trinity.

God the Father is the architect of all creation. What unfolds in history and happens in nature is the result of God the Father's purposes.

God has determined all that has happened, and all that will happen. This brings up several troubling questions. Did God create sin? The answer is "no." There is a difference between the directive will of God (those things He causes to happen), and His permissive will (those things He allows to happen). God does not desire that anyone should be eternally lost (1 Timothy 2:4). He has done everything in His power to prevent it, except override the capacity of man to choose. Yet we know that people will be eternally lost. God does not desire us to sin, but He allows us to sin. So, in saying that God has determined all that has happened and all that will happen is not to say that God created sin and is responsible for sin. But in His creation, He allowed for the possibility of sin.

God the Father was also active in the creation of the universe and world. However, so were the other members of the Trinity.

The Father Is the Author of the Plan of Salvation

God the Father established the process by which salvation would be accomplished. We see this explained clearly in Ephesians 1. God the Father determined the plan, which included our adoption as His spiritual children. Christ provided redemption for our sins through His death on the cross for us, forgave our sins, and gave us an inheritance. The Holy Spirit makes us secure in our inheritance, guarantees our salvation, and makes us eternally secure.

God the Father sent His Son into the world to redeem us. Jesus said in John 6:37–38, "All that the Father gives Me will come to Me, and the one who comes to Me I will by no means cast out. For I have come down from heaven, not to do My own will, but the will of Him who sent me."

The Father is creation's Architect.

The Father Exercises Spiritual Discipline

The Father is the disciplinarian of His children. We read in Hebrews 12:5–6, "My son, do not despise the chastening of the LORD, nor be discouraged when you are rebuked by Him; for whom the LORD loves He chastens, and scourges every son whom He receives."

All people are called the "offspring of God." In Acts 17:29, we read, "Being then the offspring of God, we ought not to think that the Divine Nature is like gold or silver or stone, an image formed by the art and thought of man." So, there is a sense in which God is the Father of all men as their Creator.

These, then, are some of the things which God the Father does that are different from the roles of God the Son and God the Holy Spirit.

The story is told of Joseph Kennedy, father of President John F. Kennedy, who once remarked of his granddaughter Caroline, Jack's daughter: "Caroline's very bright, smarter than you were, Jack, at that age."

"Yes, she is," agreed Jack. "But look who she has for a father."

And so it might be said of us, "Look who we have as a Father." No matter who our earthly father is, we have a heavenly Father who loves us, cares deeply about our welfare, and has committed His resources for our good.

FAQ #17

 How Do We Worship God the Father?

 We worship God the Father in the sincerity of our heart, ascribing with words and deeds the worth due Him.

The Spirit of Worship

All three members of the Trinity deserve our worship. While Jesus accepted the worship of others, He also encouraged worship of the Father.

In addition, we see worship distinguished between the Father and the Son in Revelation 4 and 5. In chapter 4, we see worship of the Father in heaven:

Behold, a throne was standing in heaven, and One sitting on the throne. And He who was sitting was like a jasper stone and a sardius in appearance; and there was a rainbow around the throne, like an emerald in appearance...And from the throne proceed flashes of lightning and sounds and peals of thunder. And before the throne there was, as it were, a sea of glass like crystal...The twenty-four elders will fall down before Him who sits on the throne, and will worship Him who lives forever and ever, and will cast their crowns before the throne, saying, "Worthy art Thou, our Lord and our God, to receive glory and honor and power; for Thou didst create all things, and because of Thy will they existed and were created" (Revelation 4:2, 3, 5, 6, 10, 11 NASB).

In this passage, we see God the Father worshiped as He sits in unimaginable majesty. Songs are sung to Him, praising Him for His creation. Yet in Chapter 5, we see the focus of worship turning to the Son:

Why Do I Need to Know About God the Father?

God the Father is not Jesus. Jesus is not God the Father. Neither is the Holy Spirit. God is three and yet one. That being the case, when we talk about God, sometimes we mean the triune God (all three in their triunity). But when we mean only the Father, we must understand His unique role, distinct from the other two members of the Trinity.

Behold, the Lion that is from the tribe of Judah, the Root of David, has overcome so as to open the book and its seven seals. And I saw between the throne (with the four living creatures) and the elders a Lamb standing, as if slain...And He came, and He took it out of the right hand of Him who sat on the throne. And when He had taken the book, the four living creatures and the twenty-four elders fell down before the Lamb, having each one a harp, and golden bowls full of incense, which are the prayers of the saints. And they sang a new song, saying, "Worthy art Thou to take the book, and to break its seals; for Thou wast slain, and didst purchase for God with Thy blood men from every tribe and tongue and people and nation" (Revelation 5:5, 6, 7–9, 11–12 NASB).

In this passage, we see Jesus the son being praised for giving his life to purchase the lives of those who believe in Him. Finally, we see them mentioned together:

And every created thing which is in heaven and on the earth and under the earth and on the sea, and all things in them, I heard saying, "To Him who sits on the throne, and to the Lamb, be blessing and honor and glory and dominion forever and ever" (Revelation 5:13 NASB).

While we do not want to make too great a distinction between worship of the Father and the worship of the Son, it is interesting that as you leaf through a hymnal, many of the hymns which focus on God the Father focus on His work in creation and His sovereignty over the earth, while the songs that focus on Jesus emphasize His work of salvation.

The Act of Worship

To worship God the Father is to publicly proclaim the worth due to Him. It is an activity to which all Christians are called and destined. In the Gospel of John (4:24), the Father seeks those who will worship Him in spirit and in truth. The apostle Peter wrote that we are to be a spiritual house, a holy priesthood, offering spiritual sacrifices acceptable to God through Jesus Christ (1 Peter 2:5). The Christian church was instructed to gather on the first day of the week for corporate worship. The most basic ingredients of worship in the early church were the reading and explanation of Scripture, prayer, the singing of hymns, and communion (the Lord's Supper). With the exception of the Lord's Supper, Jesus did not originate these Christian practices. They were carried over from the synagogue worship of the Jews.

The Father receives worship.

As the church matured, worship services did not change much essentially. In modern America, the emphasis on the Lord's Supper has declined significantly, being observed in some churches quarterly or twice annually, and a much greater emphasis has been placed on singing and Bible teaching.

Since no instructions are given in the Bible as to what a worship service ought to look like, the Lord apparently intended flexibility. That flexibility should be used sensitively whatever the service, it should be such that it allows full participation of the worshipers. It must be emphasized that worship is a matter of the heart. Activities must facilitate the spirit of worship in the heart and activities of the sincere believer.

SPEED BUMP

Slow down to be sure you've gotten the main points of this section.

1. Who is God the Father?
The Father is God, the first member of the Trinity.

2. **What does God the Father do?**

God the Father initiates in His relationship within the Trinity, and He provides for and protects His children.

3. **How do we worship God the Father?**

We worship God the Father in the sincerity of our heart, ascribing with words and deeds the worth due Him.

FOR FURTHER STUDY

Scriptures Passages

■ Matthew 3:17   ■ Ephesians 1:3–6
■ John 5:37   ■ Hebrews 12:9
■ Galatians 3:26

Read these passages and consider how they augment your understanding of God the Father.

FAQ #18

 What Hope Does God Give Us?

 God gives us hope in the challenges of life in this world and hope for eternal life in the next.

Hope in This Life

We need God because we need hope in this life. When life overwhelms us, when circumstances and people push us beyond our capacity to cope, we need hope. These may be times of personal upheaval. Perhaps we are facing a health crisis. Instinctively, we turn to God.

Perhaps it is a financial calamity. Or perhaps a daughter is addicted to drugs, or a son's family is tearing apart. When airplanes go down, when floodwaters come up, when calamities hit, we instinctively turn to God. We long for hope, and at such times only God can give it.

Tragedy is a great clarifier. We see truly what is important and what is not. We get in touch with our mortality and our vulnerability, and see that we need God. No force in the universe can keep people from turning to Him then. And at such times, hope is beyond the capacity of man, but God will give it.

God gives hope for both lives—now and the next.

Hope for the Next Life

We also need God because we need hope for life after death. Toward the early part of the twentieth century it became fashionable to deny the existence of God and of the afterlife. We were brave. We had a fairly stable society, which Christianity had produced. We stood bravely on that stable society and denied the God who established it. Man is only a machine. Man is only an animal.

After more than a century of that worldview we are recognizing that we are a nation in peril. We are realizing that we cannot control our own destiny in this life, let alone in the next.

People are no longer satisfied believing they are mere machines or animals. They are returning to the belief that they have souls and that there is life after death. They understand that no one has control over what happens after he dies. If anyone does control that, it would have to be God, and so people are turning to Him: Oh, God, save us, our hearts cry. Make it safe for us to die.

When I was a child I used to go swimming at a lake with a thirty-foot high-dive platform. I used to watch the other kids dive off of that

"If there were no God it would be necessary to invent Him."

Voltaire

and thought I could too. Some kids were afraid, but I wasn't. It looked simple. Exciting, even. When I climbed up the first time, I kept saying under my breath, "I'm not afraid. I'm not afraid." And I thought I wasn't.

But then I got to the top.

When I walked to the edge of the platform and looked down, thirty feet seemed like thirty miles. I was afraid. I couldn't go back, because there was a line of little lemmings on the ladder behind me, rushing to the sea, just as I was. It was one of life's most impossible moments. I couldn't go forward; I couldn't go backward. Worse, I couldn't remain where I was. Terrified, I put my mind in neutral and jumped. I nearly lost my stomach. I nearly lost my eyelids. I nearly lost my bathing suit. But I survived. On the ground before the climb it wasn't scary in the least. But up on the platform? Terrifying!

That is the way death is for those without Christ. When they are young and healthy, they aren't scared. But let them get old or sick. Get them up on the ladder with an accurate perspective, and they will be afraid. This fear is natural and God-given because it is not safe to die without God.

It takes little insight into history, into society, into our own hearts, to realize that something is wrong with humankind. It is not that we

Why I need to know that people need God:

1. If I understand why people need God, I will see more clearly why I need God.
2. If I understand why people need God, I will be able to help other people see that He is the answer to their troubles and longings.
3. If I understand why people need God and why they turn to Him, I can experience peace and comfort in turmoil, hope in uncertainty, and a calmness when facing suffering or death.

cannot do good. Clearly, we can. But it is also that we cannot keep from doing evil. The Bible says that all have sinned and come short of the glory of God (Romans 3:23). It also says that the wages of this sin is death, or separation from God forever (Romans 6:23). Therefore, forgiveness of sin and reconciliation with God is our greatest need. This forgiveness, this reconciliation, is not a complicated affair. In John 3:16, we read, "For God so loved the world that He gave His only begotten Son, that whoever believes in Him should not perish but have eternal life." "To believe," in the biblical sense, does not mean mere intellectual assent, but a personal commitment to the object of that belief. To believe in God or His Son, therefore, means to accept who He is and place yourself under His jurisdiction, to follow Him. When you do, God will respond by giving you eternal life.

So, who needs God? We all do. We need him for hope in this life and for the next.

FAQ #19

 What Moral Values Does God Give Us?

 God gives us a secure basis for truth and falsehood, and for good and evil.

We need God in order to have a secure basis for truth and morality. Years ago when I led study tours to Israel and the Middle East I took people through the Holocaust Museum in Jerusalem. As you walk through it, there are artifacts on display from the concentration camps—barbed wire, instruments of torture, scientific equipment used in conducting human experiments on the Jews, and so on. There are also thousands of pictures depicting the incomprehensible inhumanity inflicted upon the Jewish people in those concentration camps. Skeletons with skin stretched tightly over them lean against barbed wire barricades, faces staring with hollow eyes.

If it had been done to animals, it would have been an outrage. Because it was done to humans, it stands as one of the most horrible evils in the history of mankind. Holocaust: a word in the dictionary that no longer has to be explained. Everyone knows what it means. It is an event that everyone will agree was wrong. We may not agree whether abortion, capital punishment, or homosexuality are right or wrong. But we do agree that the Holocaust was wrong.

But why was it wrong?

"Why was it wrong?" you cry. "Because you can't kill people just because you don't like them."

But I could say, "The Nazis passed laws sanctioning what they did. It was all within the law. So why was it wrong if the majority of people thought that it was right?"

Right and wrong cannot exist without God.

The problem is, if you cannot appeal to an authority higher than man, you cannot use the terms "right" and "wrong." You can say you don't like it, that it's cruel, that it shouldn't be done. But that is just your opinion. You cannot say it is wrong. Hitler thought it was right. You think it is wrong. Who is correct?

One person says it is wrong to kill fetuses, and another says it is okay if the pregnancy is unwanted. Who says which one is correct?

One person says it is wrong to be sexually promiscuous, and another says it feels right. Who says which one is correct?

One person says it is wrong to steal, and another says it is allowed if we are stealing from a corporation instead of a person. Who says which one is correct?

Terms like right and wrong can be used only if there is an unchanging obligatory moral base established by God. If you do not recognize God, there is no possibility of that moral base. It is as Dostoyevsky wrote in *The Brothers Karamazov*, "If there is no God, all things are permissible."

We also need God because His truth and

morality form the basis for social stability. Without a moral base, not only do you have difficulty agreeing on morality for law and order, but you have trouble enforcing the laws you do have. There are laws against stealing, but businessmen on Wall Street steal with impunity, because they can get away with it. There are laws against bribes, graft, and kickbacks, but businesses and governments do it all the time. There are laws against drug abuse, driving while intoxicated, and pornography, and yet not enough citizens are willing to get involved to enforce these laws adequately. So social order begins to break down.

A shared view of right and wrong provides social stability.

Who needs God? We do. There is no such thing as right and wrong without Him. There can be no social order without Him. Decent life in a decent country where the innocent are protected and opportunity is secure fades away. Morality must come from a higher level, or it will sink to the lowest levels. We need to get our truth from God and make it the basis of personal and social order.

The Ten Commandments give us a powerful and unchanging underpinning for personal and social order. Found in Exodus 20:1–17, they are:

You shall have no other gods before Me.
You shall not make an idol for yourself.
You shall not take the name of the LORD your God in vain.
Remember the Sabbath day, to keep it holy.
Honor your father and your mother.
You shall not murder.
You shall not commit adultery.
You shall not steal.
You shall not bear false witness.
You shall not covet.

If these moral laws were observed, most personal and social evils could be avoided. These powerful truths for personal and social order come from the lips of God. Who needs God? Everyone who wants a society that functions with fairness and justice needs Him.

FAQ #20

 What Does God Give Us to Live For?

 God satisfies the deepest longings of our souls.

There are many longings of the human soul, but two of the deepest are the longings for love and purpose. These are longings which God gave us, because He wants to be the One to fulfill them. In fact, He is the only One who can satisfy them fully.

However, most of us tend to look to people and things in this world for the satisfaction of these longings. On one level this is natural, because even God uses people and things in this world to contribute the satisfaction of our longings. And, as long as things go well for us, this is a deceptively effective strategy. However, most of us cannot control people and things completely enough to be fully satisfied all the time. In fact, we are often unfulfilled much of the time.

Looking at the first longing for love, we find ourselves doing the very thing that destroys our love. We are obsessed with winning, with being number one, with getting life to go our way. Because of this drive to "succeed" we tend to see other people either as obstacles to our goals or as resources to be used in the pursuit of our goals. We either fight people or use them. As a result, many have lost the art of loving. Husbands do not know how to love their wives. Wives do not know how to love their husbands. Parents do not know how to love their children, and, therefore, children do not know how to love their parents. Co-workers, neighbors, relatives do not know how to love each other.

This breakdown in knowing how to love results in loneliness. We don't feel loved; therefore, we feel lonely. Today, even the "traditional" family is often no longer a unit, but a collection of individuals living under the same roof. Each one has his own bedroom, his own television and stereo, and each one has his own activity schedule. This is a certain recipe for loneliness. We seek more privacy and yet feel more alienated and lonely when we get it.

Looking at the longing for purpose, we discover that we are, again, doing the very thing that keeps us from having a sense of purpose. We were never created to live for ourselves. We were created to live for other people and for causes that are greater than ourselves. However, we spend our lives chasing material comfort and possessions, and we find there is no satisfying sense of purpose in selfish living. Therefore, to mask the sense of purposelessness and loneliness combined, we turn to work, alcohol, drugs, sex, sensual entertainment, Satanism and witchcraft, and to an alarming degree, we even commit suicide. Why? Because the things we live for don't satisfy.

Only God can satisfy the deepest longing of our soul.

The bumper sticker says, "The one who dies with the most toys wins." What a foolish philosophy! My guess is that the phrase was coined by someone who thinks he is running a race, but he will find out he is walking off a gangplank.

Though there are more people in the world than ever before, people are lonelier than ever before. And though we are a richer nation than ever before, never have more of our citizens experienced such an acute lack of purpose.

THINKING BACK

God is our solution to our longing for love. He first loves us and, by demonstration and then by teaching through the Scriptures, He shows us how to love others. First John 4:19 says, "We love God because He first loved us." That is the pattern for meaningful relationships. Others will love us as they perceive that we first love them. Whether it is in the family, the church, or society as a whole, others love us as they perceive our love for them. Selfishness, isolation, striving for success, being number one, all these militate against love. If we'll do it His way, God can help us love and feel loved while here on earth.

However, this world is not a perfect place. Our families may be dysfunctional, our friends unfaithful, our co-workers disloyal. Even when friends fail us in this life, we can turn to the Lord who loves us without limit and without end. He values us if no one else does. We can receive emotional support from God Himself to help us grieve through the pain of lost love in this life. And beyond that, we can look forward to eternity when God will love us and we will love God face to face. At the same time, we will be surrounded in heaven by God's children of all ages who will also love us perfectly. We will belong to a great spiritual family and never feel lonely again.

In addition, God is our solution to our longing for purpose. As we turn from living for ourselves to living for others and living for the advancement of heaven's influence on earth, we begin to have a deep sense of purpose. President John Kennedy once said, "Ask not what your country can do for you. Ask what you can do for your country." In principle, God asks the same of us. We ask, not what others can do for us, but what we can do for others. In that pursuit, we find a sense of purpose in this life.

Not only does God give us a sense of purpose in this life, but He also holds out to us a sense of purpose throughout eternity. We will rule and reign with Him in heaven forever. We will be gifted for great service to and with Him. We will accomplish more good in eternity than our minds have the ability to imagine.

In Matthew 22:37–39, Jesus said, "'You shall love the LORD your God with all your heart, with all your soul, and with all your mind.' This is the great and foremost commandment. And a second is like it, 'You shall love your neighbor as yourself.'" These commandments are the keys to meeting our deepest longings for love and purpose.

God is the ultimate answer for the deep longings of our soul, both in this life and in the life to come. Who needs

God? We do—for love and for purpose, to fulfill the deepest longings of our soul.

It is as C. S. Lewis, a British Christian scholar who died in 1964, once wrote, speaking of the relationship between living for this world and living for the next world: "Shoot for the heaven, and you get earth thrown in. Shoot for earth and you get neither."

Who needs God? We all do.

SPEED BUMP!

Slow down to be sure you've gotten the main points of this section.

1. What hope does God give us?
God gives us hope in the challenges of life in this world and hope for eternal life in the next.

2. What moral values does God give us?
God gives us a secure basis for truth and falsehood, and for good and evil.

3. What does God give us to live for?
God satisfies the deepest longings of our souls.

FOR FURTHER STUDY

Scripture Passages

- Proverbs 1:20–33
- Acts 17:16–34
- Romans 1:18–2:2
- 1 Corinthians 15:12–19
- Galatians 5:19–23

Read these passages and consider how they contribute to your understanding of humanity's need for God.

FAQ #21

 How Can We Learn About God?

 We learn about God through the Bible, through nature, and through our conscience.

God has given us three primary ways to know about Him. First, through the Bible. Even atheists can learn about the God they don't believe in by reading the Bible. They can know that if this God did exist, this is what He would be like. Most of us learn about God initially from well-known Bible stories—Moses and the Exodus, David and Goliath, Daniel in the lions' den, Jesus' miracles or parables, the Crucifixion and the Resurrection, and so on. Even if you watch television quiz shows you will see questions about these stories. And as we learn more about the Bible, we will discover about more of God's power, intelligence, presence, love, justice, compassion, even His wrath. We learn about God from the Bible.

A second source for learning about God is "nature." In the Bible we read that "what may be known of God is manifest...for God has shown it to them...For since the creation of the world His invisible attributes...His eternal power and Godhead—are clearly seen, being understood by the things that are made" (Romans 1:19–20).

Abraham Lincoln once said, "I can see how it might be possible for a man to look down upon the earth and be an atheist, but I cannot conceive how he could look up into the heavens and say there is no God." We see that He is a God of stupendous power and magnitude. when we look for the first time at the Grand Canyon, or Yosemite Valley, or Rocky Mountain National Park. We learn about God from nature.

> "God is like a person who clears His throat while hiding and so gives himself away."
>
> *Meister Eckhardt*

A third avenue for learning about God is through our conscience plus reflection. The Bible tells us that God put eternity into the heart of man (Ecclesiastes 3:11). That is, He has created man with a capacity to look for, long for, understand, and embrace the divine. When one reflects on truth with this innate knack for the eternal, one can learn about God.

We learn about God through the Bible.

The question is, "What do you do with this information?" You will either move toward God or away from Him. If you move toward Him, you can meet Him. If you move away from Him, or (from your viewpoint) stand still, you will not meet Him.

FAQ #22

How Do We Meet God?

We meet God by saying "yes" to God's invitation to come to Him.

God says that He loves us (John 3:16). He reveals a lot of other information about Himself in the Scripture, nature, and through our conscience. "Will you be my child?" He asks.

This is more remarkable than any marriage proposal because God is so far above us. Nevertheless, will we accept His offer? Like the courted lover, we have the power to say "no." But if we say "yes," we are united with Him forever.

It is unlike the human relationship, however, in that, when a woman refuses a marriage proposal, she may find someone else. Nothing bad will necessarily happen to her if she rejects him. Something even better might happen. Rejecting God however, is the gravest of all human acts. To be separated from God forever is unthinkable to those who understand the implications.

But, back to the question, "How can we meet God?" First, we

must understand He asks us to come to Him. "Behold, I stand at the door and knock; If anyone hears My voice and opens the door, I will come in to him and dine with him, and he with Me" (Revelation 3:20). This invitation of fellowship with God reveals His desire for a close relationship with us.

Then, we must say "yes" to the invitation to enter into a relationship with Him. If we do, it means that we are no longer masters of our own lives.

Maybe you are familiar with the poem "Invictus":

Out of the night that covers me,
Black as the Pit from pole to pole,
I thank whatever gods may be
For my unconquerable soul.

In the fell clutch of circumstance,
I have not winced nor cried aloud;
Under the bludgeonings of chance
My head is bloody, but unbowed.

It matters not how straight the gate,
How charged with punishment the scroll.
I am the master of my fate;
I am the captain of my soul.

William Ernest Hensley

When I first read that poem, as a new Christian, it stirred me in a way that is difficult to put into words. I longed to have control over my life and had the momentary illusion that I could. But soon I began to see that the words were sheer idiocy. It seemed like a man who stands before a benevolent king, being offered half the kingdom in return for homage, and the man says, "Forget it, I am the master of my fate, I am the captain of my soul," and promptly throws himself into the mouth

of a volcano. So you are the master of your fate, captain of your soul!
What virtue is there in being captain of your soul if it results in your
destruction?

God beckons us, like a suitor, to His love. We answer "yes"
or "no." If "yes," our new relationship entails certain
changes. We are no longer our own masters. We must
adjust ourselves to the requirements of Him who is
Lord. We cannot say "yes" to God and "no" to
all He stands for, any more than a woman
could accept a man's marriage proposal,
and then still see other men, refuse to
keep house with him, and refuse to bear or
care for their children. When we say "yes" to
God, we say "yes" to all we understand of His expectations for us.

> **We meet God by saying yes to Him.**

It may be that, after having said "yes," we learn about an
expectation He had for us that we did not understand in the
beginning. That often throws Christians into crisis. The most common one is that God does not eliminate the suffering of Christians.
But that expectation and disappointment is worked through with
God's help, just as things unforeseen in a marriage are worked
through after the ceremony.

How do we meet God? We say "yes" to His invitation, and give
ourselves to Him. It is the starting point for knowing God.

Why Do I Need To Know God?

1. If I do not know God, my soul is lost forever.
2. If I do not know God, I have no ultimate answers for my
   deepest questions and longings.
3. If I do not know God, I have no lasting truth, guidance, and
   comfort in life's trials.
4. If I do not know God, I have no biblical answers to give to
   others in their difficulties and questionings.

FAQ #23

 How Can We Grow in Our Relationship with God?

 We grow in our relationship with God when we learn of God's character and commands, and then trust and obey Him.

Growing in our relationship with God involves learning what He asks of us and doing our best to accomplish it. Specifically, learning involves reading the Bible with an attitude of compliance, looking to see how our lives might not match what is taught, and then striving to align ourselves with the truth.

First Peter 2:2 says we should be as newborn babes who "desire the milk of the word," that we might grow in respect to salvation. As we give serious attention to heeding the Scripture, we will grow and mature as Christians. Romans 6:17 reads, "But God be thanked that though you were slaves of sin, yet you obeyed from the heart that form of doctrine to which you were delivered." The Roman Christians were not obedient with gritted teeth or clenched fists. They were obedient from the heart, which is what God asks of us. In his marvelous book *Knowing God*, J. I. Packer lists four activities through which we know God:

We grow in our relationship with God by obeying Him.

1. Listening to God's Word and receiving it as the Holy Spirit interprets it in application to oneself.
2. Noting God's nature and character, as His Word and works reveal it.

3. **Accepting His invitations, and doing what He commands.**
4. **Recognizing, and rejoicing in, the love that He has shown in drawing one into this divine fellowship. (32).**

We might summarize this as:

1. **Honoring God's Word.**
2. **Trusting God's character.**
3. **Obeying Him.**
4. **Enjoying Him.**

We have already looked at honoring God's Word, so let's now look at why trusting God's character is essential for growth. If we are to grow, we must trust God, especially when that means obeying Him in the difficult things.

I enjoy some of the old black-and-white movies based on classic literature. In the 1940 version of "The Mark of Zorro", Tyrone Power plays the "Robin Hood of California" in a fairly faithful production of the original book. In the movie, there is a remarkable chase scene in which Zorro is fleeing in the dead of night from a band of Spanish army officers. He is dressed in black, and his horse, of course, is jet black. Racing at breakneck speed through woods, over creeks, along narrow paths, Zorro is finally cornered on a bridge suspended about twenty feet over a river. In one of the most remarkable stunts I have ever seen in a movie, the rider (probably not Tyrone Power) turned the horse toward the railing on the bridge, which was about four-and-a-half feet high, and spurred him. The horse jumped over the railing, into the river below, with the rider still on him. It swam downstream in a hail of bullets from the bridge, and once again, Zorro made a cunning escape.

My question is, how in the world did that stunt rider get that horse to jump over that railing into the black abyss below? That is one of the most unnatural things a horse would ever do. A horse would be almost as likely to dance ballet or swim a backstroke as to jump into a black abyss.

I learned the answer from those who train horses. The secret is that the rider must never ask the horse to do anything that hurts it. The rider first gets the horse to do little stunts that seem dangerous, but the horse does not get hurt. So the trainer graduates to stunts of medium difficulty and danger. Finally, he graduates to major stunts. After years of training, the horse learns to trust the rider, because nothing traumatizing has ever happened to him in the past. As a result, he will do almost anything the rider asks of him in the future. Obviously, this rider had spent a lot of time working with that horse, and had developed a high degree of trust. The horse never hesitated—over the rail and into the river.

We grow in God by enjoying Him.

That is where God wants to get us. He wants to get us to the point at which we will go off a cliff for Him if we understand that He is the one who is asking. The only way we will ever do that is if we learn to deeply trust His character.

Trust leads us to "accepting His invitations and doing what He commands." Jesus said, "Come to Me, all you who labor and are heavy laden, and I will give you rest. Take My yoke upon you and learn from Me, for I am gentle and lowly in heart, and you will find rest for your souls. For My yoke is easy, and My burden is light" (Matthew 11:28–30). What an invitation! How we would grow if we were to accept it. I have found that whenever life's load is getting too heavy for me to bear, I am trying to carry something Jesus never intended for me to carry. I am taking up a yoke which only He can bear. When I lay that yoke down, life gets bearable again. Let me explain.

A little over a year before the writing of this book, I came down with a serious illness. I had to leave the church I was pastoring because I had become disabled and, more than a year later, I was still unable to pastor. It was easy to become worried about the future. Who's going to pay the bills? Would I ever be well enough to function normally again? Is the rest of the world going to forget about me? Will I ever be able to pastor a church again? Will I be in dreadful physical pain the rest of my life? Would I ever be able to live as I had before?

The evil one took these matchboxes of worry, struck them, and fanned them into an inferno of insecurity and anxiety. Time and time again, I would read Matthew 6:27–34:

Which of you by worrying can add one cubit to his stature? So why do you worry about clothing? Consider the lilies of the field how they grow: they neither toil nor spin; and yet I say to you that even Solomon in all his glory was not arrayed like one of these. Now if God so clothes the grass of the field, which today is, and tomorrow is thrown into the oven, will He not much more clothe you, O you of little faith? Therefore do not worry, saying, 'What shall we eat?' or 'What shall we drink?' or 'What shall we wear?' For after all these things the Gentiles seek. For your heavenly Father knows that you need all these things. But seek first the kingdom of God and His righteousness, and all these things shall be added to you. Therefore do not worry about tomorrow, for tomorrow will worry about its own things. Sufficient for the day is its own trouble.

When I would read this passage, I knew that I was carrying a burden which Jesus never intended me to carry. If I would come to Him, and lay the burden down, I could find rest for my soul. It wasn't easy, and I didn't execute it perfectly, but at least I understood that if I could bring myself to trust God, I could stop worrying. That is what Packer means by accepting God's invitations.

"Doing what He commands" is tied closely to accepting His invitations. We obey God when we believe what He says. When we don't believe, we don't obey. If we fully believed that God commands only what is for our benefit and prohibits only what would harm us, we would never flagrantly disobey Him. Because of our creaturely weakness, in the face of temptation we have not caused, we might trip up and fall, but we would not disobey Him with malice and forethought.

Trusting and obeying God opens the door to the delights of "recognizing and rejoicing in the love He has shown in drawing us into His divine fellowship." This opportunity may be hard for us to appreciate if we do not grasp the significance of what God has done. The poet Carl Sandburg once said, "Without great audiences, there can be no great poets." An audience must have the capacity to recognize greatness before a great poet will ever get the recognition he deserves. So true. In the analogy, God is the Great Poet and we are the audience. If we do not recognize the greatness of the Poet, He will not get the recognition from us that He deserves. However, as we grow in our capacity to recognize and appreciate His greatness, we learn to rejoice in what God has done for us. Even in the firestorms of life, we can smile with joy as we enjoy God.

We grow in our relationship with God by trusting Him.

THINKING BACK

In this world we cannot know God in exactly the same way we know a human being. Another human being looks into our eyes as we speak and talks to us in return. We get clear and immediate answers to our questions. Body language, facial expressions, and vocal inflections tell us what the other person is thinking and feeling. The level of communication allows us to have a degree of emotional intimacy that is often not possible with God. Having a relationship with God is like relating to a person whose face you cannot see, who does not talk with you aloud, and in whose voice you cannot read humor or sadness. On the other hand, we can know God, and He does communicate to us. There is a spiritual intimacy we can have with Him that we cannot have with another person, because God has answers that people do not have, and God gives comfort and hope that people cannot give.

When I was terribly sick and in dreadful pain, it was God to whom I turned. My dear wife, Margie, was a source of God's grace for which I shall be eternally grateful, but even she could not do what God did for me. I turned to Him again and again, often in tears, pleading with God to take away the pain. I read and read the Psalms and saw that David was not shy about telling God how he hurt. He even pleaded with God to take away the pain. If David could do it, so could I. I also read the Crucifixion account over and over. Jesus suffered so much for me, and I had no capacity to grasp just how much until I had had a good taste of suffering myself. I clung to the promise that His grace would be sufficient for me (2 Corinthians 12:9). Often, I did not feel that it was. But as I look back, it must have been because here I am.

I also contemplated the throne room chapters in Revelation 4 and 5. I took consolation in the hope of one day being there and singing His praises without pain.

The holiness of God also became a vivid concept to me, and a terribly important one. Somehow my pain helped me understand and appreciate His holiness more than ever. Night was always the worst time. There were many evenings when I thought I just couldn't stand to go through another night. And yet the nights came, and I was still alive, so what option was there but to go through them? In whispers I would quote the great "holiness" chapter of the Bible, Isaiah 6:1–8. When I finished that, I would softly sing the hymn, "Holy, Holy, Holy, Lord God Almighty! Early in the morning our song shall rise to Thee; Holy, holy, holy! merciful and mighty! God in three persons, blessed Trinity." After I had sung all four stanzas I would start over with Isaiah 6. When I had finished Isaiah 6, I would sing "Holy, Holy, Holy" again, until I finally fell asleep.

Somehow, in the middle of the pain and the distress, God was there. I did not "feel" His presence, but I was comforted by Him in a way that no human could have comforted me.

So, we cannot know God in exactly the same way we know other human beings, but we can know God in a way that we cannot know other human beings. We must never demand to know

God in exactly the same way that we know other people. We must seek God, and we can know Him, in a way that we cannot know other people. We know Him by learning about Him, by approaching Him in faith, by seeking to align our lives with whatever we understand He requires of us, and by clinging to Him in the difficult times.

SPEED BUMP!

Slow down to be sure you've gotten the main points of this section.

1. How can we learn about God?
We learn about God through the Bible, through nature, and through our conscience.

2. How can we meet God?
We meet God by saying "yes" to God's invitation to come to Him.

3. How can we grow in our relationship with God?
We grow in our relationship with God when we learn of God's character and commands, and then trust and obey Him.

FOR FURTHER STUDY

Scripture Passages
A number of important passages address the subject of knowing God:

- John 17:13
- Acts 22:14
- 1 Corinthians 1:21
- 1 Corinthians 2:9–16
- Galatians 4:8–9

- Ephesians 3:14–19
- 1 John 4:6–8
- 1 John 5:2
- 1 John 5:20

Passages dealing with suffering include:

- **Philippians 4:10**
- **James 1:2–5**
- **1 Peter 2:19–24**
- **1 Peter 3:8–9**

Read these passages for additional information on knowing God.

FAQ #24

 What Is Our Greatest Natural Desire?

 Our greatest natural desire is to be happy.

God created us with deep longings that drive our thoughts and actions. Different people express it in various ways, but our ultimate search is for happiness. We do the things we believe will make us happy.

Blaise Pascal saw that

All men seek happiness. This is without exception. Whatever different means they employ, they all tend to this end. The cause of some going to war, and of others avoiding it, is the same desire in both, attended with different views. The will never takes the least step but to this object. This is the motive of every action of every man, even of those who hang themselves (Pascal's *Pensées* p. 113).

"Lord, give me one hundred men who hate nothing but sin, and desire nothing but God, and I will shake the world."

John Wesley

Some Christians have trouble accepting that, because we have this vague notion that it is not proper to want happiness. It sounds selfish. However, it may very well be that God created us for happiness. If so, it would not be wrong for us to want it. All that would remain would be for us to determine how we pursue happiness. If we pursue God and His purposes for creation, our longings will never be too great.

C. S. Lewis once wrote

that if there lurks in most modern minds the notion that to desire our own good and earnestly to hope for the enjoyment of it is a bad thing, I submit that this notion has crept in from Kant [a major German philosopher] and the Stoics [ancient Greek philosophers] and is no part of the Christian faith. Indeed, if we consider the unblushing promises of reward and the staggering nature of the rewards promised in the Gospels, it would seem that Our Lord finds our desires not too strong, but too weak. We are half-hearted creatures, fooling about with drink and sex and ambition when infinite joy is offered to us, like an ignorant child who wants to go on making mud pies in a slum because he cannot imagine what is

People to Know

Blaise Pascal: (1623–1662) French mathematician, scientist and religious thinker; one of the greatest minds in Western intellectual history. His writings on religious subjects contain some of the most profound thinking in modern history.

C. S. Lewis: (1898–1962) British scholar and brilliant Christian thinker, writer, novelist, teacher at Oxford and Cambridge. His Christian books have sold more copies than any other author in history.

meant by the offer of a holiday at the sea. We are far too easily
pleased (*The Weight of Glory and Other Addresses*, pp. 1–2).

There is no vice in admitting our longings. We want to be happy.
Now. How does that desire stack up with Scripture?

Happiness, or some other synonym that we might choose, such
as joy, or meaning, or satisfaction, is the sole intent of Christendom.
Listen as the Scriptures speak.

John 10:10 (Jesus is speaking of those who believe in Him): "I
have come that they may have life, and that they may have it
more abundantly."

Matthew 5:8: "Happy are the pure in heart, for they shall see
God" (NASB).

Galatians 5:22: "The fruit of the Spirit is love, joy, peace..."

Psalm 37:4: "Delight yourself also in the Lord/And He shall give
you the desires of your heart."

Psalm 36:8: "[Men] drink their fill of the abun-
dance of thy house; and thou dost give
them to drink of the river of thy
delights" (NASB).

Psalm 34:8: "Oh, taste and see
that the LORD is good."

Psalm 16:11: "In thy presence is fullness of joy; in
thy right hand there are pleasures forever" (NASB).

God created us with a deep desire for true happiness.

Happiness, joy, and pleasure are not illegitimate experiences in
the Christian life; they are central to God's intentions. Most of us
have a right to be much happier than we are.

So step number one in the pursuit of God is to admit our longings.

FAQ #25

 Q **What Are the Most Dangerous Counterfeits?**

 A **The most dangerous counterfeits of happiness are money, beauty, and talent.**

It is all right to desire happiness and joy. God created us with those longings. But He also created us so that He is the only one who can fulfill them. We err when we go outside of Him to try to fulfill our yearnings.

Blaise Pascal went on to write:

There once was in man a true happiness of which now remain to him only the dark and empty trace, which he in vain tries to fill from all his surroundings, seeking from things absent the help he does not find in things present. But these are all inadequate, because the infinite abyss can only be filled by an infinite and immutable object, that is to say, only by God Himself (Pascal's *Pensées* p. 113).

We must deeply believe that God is the source of all true and lasting happiness. We were created by God for God and we will not find our happiness until we find it in God. Yet this takes us 180 degrees opposite our natural inclinations in our pursuit of happiness.

What do we more naturally depend on to bring us happiness? Money is perhaps the number one thing. Beauty is another. Talent is a third.

Money

Money gives status and brings power and freedom. Many of you would say that you have difficulty thinking of anything you need that money would not help. Perhaps you have been where I have been before. I had my health. I had a wife who loved me. I had a job that I found meaning in. But if I just had more money! Everything would be perfect then.

Money **may help provide some basic needs, but it cannot make us happy.**

Yet, money can be an opiate. It may be like cocaine. The more you have the more you may want, so that no matter how much you have, you still may not have enough. Therefore, money does not satisfy. Benjamin Franklin once said that:

Money never made a man happy yet, nor will it. There is nothing in its nature to produce happiness. The more a man has, the more he wants. Instead of its filling a vacuum, it makes one. If it satisfies one want, it doubles and trebles that want another way. That was a true proverb of the wise man: rely upon it: "Better is little with the fear of the Lord, than great treasures, and trouble therewith."

In most cases, if you are not happy without money, you will not be happy with it. Money is often necessary for things we actually need, but if we look to it to make us happy, it fails us. As the source of happiness, even genuine money is a counterfeit—a mirage. Yet we all pursue and long for it perhaps more than anything else. But it is a starving substitute for God.

Solomon said in the Proverbs: "Wealth is worthless in the day of wrath, but righteousness delivers from death" (11:4 NASB). "Do not wear yourself out to get rich; have the wisdom to show restraint. Cast but a glance at riches, and they are gone, for they will surely spout wings and fly off to the sky like an eagle" (23:4–5 NASB).

Beauty

We pursue beauty because we think that by looking nice, we can get people to like us. Now there is nothing wrong with looking nice. But if you are obsessed with it, if you are not content to look as nice as you do naturally, if you feel you must spend inordinate time and money to look nice, then you have a problem.

Physical **beauty always fades and cannot make us truly happy.**

If we are basing our happiness on people's acceptance of us because of how we look, we are setting ourselves up for disappointment. God has made us to look the way we look, and has done so for a reason. Therefore, He plans to give us a meaningful life no matter how we look. Our goal in life should not be to be so concerned with our appearance that we are willing to look or act unspiritually to gain others' attention. Our goal in life should be to ask God what it is that He wants to do in and through our lives, given the physical body He has given us.

Talent

Talent is similar to beauty. It is a wonderful servant or a terrible master. If we place our sense of worth on talents we possess, we become shallow and insecure, fearing the day our talent fails us. If we equate intelligence as a kind of talent, the same rule applies.

Only God can give us what we truly long for. In wanting money and beauty and talent, we are really longing for love and belonging, on one hand, and meaning and purpose on the other. Only God can love us fully. Our spouse may fail us. Our family may misunderstand us. Friends may turn away. But God will never fail us. If we look to God to fund our emotional checking account, we can remain steady and strong when others fail us. If we are secure in God's love, our spouse can fail to love us, but we can keep on loving him or her. If we are secure in God's love, our family can misunderstand us, but we can keep on loving them. If we are secure in God's love, friends can turn away, but we can keep on loving them.

And our spouse, family members, and our friends will die. But God will not die. If we are secure in God's love, we can remain unbroken when loved ones die. While we may be terribly lonely, we can live in anticipation for the day we will be reunited with our loved ones, because God will bring it to pass.

Only God can love us perfectly and unendingly. Only God can meet our ultimate need for love and security and acceptance.

And as for meaning and purpose and satisfaction? Only God can give us that. What job gives us ultimate meaning and satisfaction? What accomplishment lasts? I remember when I learned that my first book would be published. I received the call from the publisher around noon. After I hung up, I jumped up and down in the middle of the room and shouted for probably two minutes. Then I did a jig and began skipping around the perimeter of the room. Finally, I danced into the middle again and repeated my original performance of jumping straight up and down, whooping and hollering.

That joy lasted for about a week. Then life resumed its usual course. Now that I have written a number of books, the thrill lasts for

Why Do I Need To Know This?

1. Unless you understand that only God can satisfy your fundamental drive to be happy, you could easily spend your entire life looking for happiness elsewhere.

2. You could not only miss out on happiness in this life, but on eternal life, also.

3. You must understand that desiring God is not enough. You must also stop doing the things that drive a wedge between you and God or else your relationship with Him will never flourish. It like physical fitness: Not only must you eat a good diet, but you must also stop harmful habits—smoking, drinking, worrying, stressing your body, and getting no exercise and too little sleep.

4. Unless you follow these principles, you will be of little help to others who are struggling. The ministry you long to have to others will not exist because you will not have any answers.

about ten minutes before the reality sets in.

What job will give you ultimate fulfillment? You work your head off, and the people you work for don't appreciate it or reward you sufficiently. You give your money away to people, and they come to expect it. You pour your life into your children and they have no capacity to appreciate what you do for them. Don't get me wrong. It is right and good to take meaning in the things you do, but you cannot build your whole life on them. They will fail you.

But God—God doesn't fail you. The one thing that can give ultimate and permanent meaning in life is to know that when you go to bed at night, you lived that day, as best you knew how, for God. If that anchors your life, the winds of adversity can blow and the vicissitudes of life can take their unexpected turns. It doesn't matter. You are anchored to a Rock that will not move. You are secure.

alent, like money and even beauty, is a wonderful servant, but a terrible master.

God may give us great meaning and satisfaction in people and in our jobs. He may have made us beautiful or handsome. We may get much fulfillment from life. But if we are not living for the Lord, we crash and burn when life fails us. If we are living for the Lord, we may crash, but we don't burn. We can rise again. We must recognize the counterfeits we live for; call them what they are, and live for the things which alone can give ultimate satisfaction.

FAQ #26

 What Is the Source of True Happiness?

 God alone is the source of true happiness.

After we have admitted that we have a deep longing for happiness—a longing for love and acceptance and security on the one hand, and purpose and meaning and satisfaction on the other—we must choose things of true value, and reject things that are false.

When we feel lonely and rejected and yearn for someone to affirm us, it is heaven that we long for; it is God whom we seek. When we are tired and defeated and crave a taste of success, it is heaven that we long for; it is God whom we seek. When we seem hollow and empty inside, struggling for meaning and purpose in life, it is heaven that we long for; it is God whom we seek.

Surely, God will give us people and circumstances which help us from time to time to feel accepted and to have meaning in life. But what happens when all fails us? What do we do when life collapses in on top of us? We have a protection. In the tempest we have safe harbor. In the darkest night, we have a compass. God will see us through if (and it is a big if) we have given ourselves to Him and have learned to take our love and purpose from Him. Life may hurt us, but with God in our hearts, it will not destroy us.

Listen to what Paul wrote in 2 Corinthians 4:8–10:

nly God can provide true happiness.

We are afflicted in every way, but not crushed; perplexed but not despairing; persecuted, but not forsaken; struck down, but not destroyed; always carrying about in the body the dying of Jesus, that the life of Jesus also may be manifested in our body (NASB).

The price of choosing God, is, of course, total. Choosing God costs all that we have and all that we are. In return, God promises to fulfill the deepest longings of our soul. He promises to satisfy us with Himself.

We admit our deep longings, we recognize the inadequacy of counterfeits, and we choose God. That is the basis upon which we pursue God. In our great longings in life, ultimately, it is heaven that we long for. It is God whom we seek.

FAQ #27

What Must We Guard in Our Pursuit of God?

In our pursuit of God, we must guard our
spiritual disciplines, pur enviornment, and
our friends.

Engaging in "religious activities" is not the same as pursuing God.
You can engage in religious activities with a heart of stone. Many people do. You can engage in religious activities with a heart inflamed
with lust. Many people do. Participating in religious activities guarantees nothing. On the other hand, if you have a heart sensitive toward
God or want to develop one, there are certain "religious-looking" activities you must engage in. Just because you do them doesn't mean you
are pursuing God, but if you are pursuing God, you must do them.

We Must Guard Our Spiritual Disciplines

First, you must pray. The very heart of pursuing God is talking to
Him. You should not only have regular times for prayer, you should culti-
vate a habit of going to God throughout the day in prayer as though you
were conversing with someone at your side. Actually He is closer than
that. He is within you.

Another thing you must do is learn your Bible.
Notice I did not say read or study, because they are
often too simplistic. You must read and study,
but you must also hear good preaching
and be involved in a Bible study with
a good teacher. All four things, at least.
Reading good Christian books, taking Christian
study courses by tape or correspondence, and other
similar activities help you learn your Bible. Jesus said,
"You shall know the truth, and the truth will set you free."
That means that if you remain ignorant of the Bible, you will be in
bondage; bondage to bad decisions, foolish desires, to unhelpful atti-
tudes, and so on. You must learn the Bible.

Spiritual

disciplines help us

pursue God.

You must also worship with other believers. In most cases, this means going to church, though there are rare exceptions where that is not always possible. You may be a missionary in a Muslim country where there is no church to go to. But you can worship God nevertheless. The typical person in the United States, however, is spiritually obligated to find the best church he can find, connect with the most spiritual people in it, and try to make it an even better church.

Pursuing God means that you will attempt to live a life of service to others. There are those who are not Christians, and you can share the gospel message with them. There are those in need and you may be able to help in Jesus' name. Other Christians may need the benefit of your God-given gifts. Jesus said that if you would keep your life, you must lose it. He meant, primarily, that one must relinquish his life to the authority of Jesus, and implied that we must live for others, not merely for ourselves.

Our living environment may help or hinder our pursuit of God.

The Lord will give you many opportunities to pursue Him. If your heart is in pursuit, you will find a hundred disciplines to help.

We Must Control Our Living Environment

You frequently will hear sociologists contend that "we are products of our environment." As Christians who are committed to pursuing God, we believe that there are many more factors that shape who we are. Yet the influence of environment is inescapable. If we live and work in a pigpen, we will smell like a pigpen. It may not actually turn us into pigs, but we will carry their aroma around with us.

Computer programmers coined the phrase "Garbage in, garbage out." By this they mean that the end product will only be as good as what goes into it. Data that is incomplete or distorted will inevitably produce results that are skewed. No amount of manipulation will make the outcome any better.

Recognizing the importance of environment, we should strive to place ourselves in places and situations that will affect us positively. Conversely, we should seek to avoid places and situations that will bring us down. To a larger degree than we often wish to acknowledge, the environments within which we operate are a matter of choice. If we choose to work in a flower shop, we may come out smelling like a rose!

We Must Control Our Relationships

When I was in college a friend of mine associated himself for a while with a "fast" crowd. He didn't drink alcohol, but most of the people in this group did. Eventually he realized that other people on campus were identifying him with the lifestyle of his associates simply because they were together so much.

In our choice of friends, we choose who influences us in our pursuit of God.

Young people, in particular, struggle with how much contact to have with the world. How can we give a Christian witness to people we never meet? It is true that our witness is limited if we spend all of our time within the "cocoon" of our church family. It is certainly true that Jesus regularly dined and otherwise associated with "sinners." We must remember, though, that He was operating from a position of strength few of us can claim. He knew who He was and what His mission was. He dealt with "sinners" in light of that identity and sense of purpose. We have been charged with continuing His mission, but we must guard against relating to people in the world in ways that drag us down or pull us away from our pursuit of God.

THINKING BACK

As I mentioned earlier, Margie and I have gone off desserts except for certain holidays and days that are special to us. One of those days is the Fourth of July. One Fourth of July we decided to celebrate by going down to a special restaurant for their five-nut brownie with vanilla ice cream on top. We dreamed of that dessert. We decided weeks ahead of time that we would get a bowl of baked potato soup and split it. Then we would get one of their special salads and split it. Then we would each get a five-nut brownie. We didn't want to be so full that dinner spoiled our dessert.

We ate the baked potato soup. It was all that we hoped for. We ate the special chicken salad. It was everything we remembered. Then came the five-nut brownie we had anticipated so long. We each got one. We looked at them for a second. We lifted them up and smelled them. Then, we dug in. Each of us took a big bite of brownie and ice cream, and, as we swallowed, we almost choked. It was so sweet and so rich, it overwhelmed us. Not easily dissuaded, we pretended it wasn't really so bad, and we plowed into another bite. We almost gagged. Awash in denial and desperately wanting to enjoy it, we took one final bite. It was all over. We were defeated. We threw down our spoons. The five-nut brownies remained on our plate as we paid our bill and walked out the door. We went home and I had a bowl of granola.

As we pursue God, He will change our tastes. He will lessen our taste for the things the world finds enjoyable but not fulfilling. And He will satisfy us with Himself. Imagine that you are adrift in the ocean without any water. In that situation, it is not wrong for you to be thirsty. You were created to need water. You were created to develop a deep, driving thirst if you go too long without water. But you must drink pure water. To drink salt water does not satisfy the craving that drove you to drink it in the first place. Rather, it will dehydrate you and hasten your death.

And so it is with the emotional longings that drive so many of us. We long for love and acceptance, meaning and purpose. It is not wrong for us to long for them. We were created to long for them. God has created us to value these things. But He also created us so that He, and He alone, can satisfy these longings. Only in Christ can we have these longings gratified. We find ourselves adrift in life, floating on a sea of money, and sex, and ambition, and pleasure. We think that by drinking them, we will slake our thirst for love and acceptance and meaning and purpose. Not so. They are all saltwater.

As we pursue God, He will change our tastes.

Do you have unfulfilled longings in life? It is heaven that you long for. It is God whom you seek. Do not pursue these counterfeits that do not satisfy. Pursue God.

SPEED BUMP!

Slow down to be sure you've gotten the main points of this section.

1. What is our greatest natural desire?
Our greatest natural desire is to be happy.

2. What are the most dangerous counterfeits?
The most dangerous counterfeits of happiness are money, beauty, and talent.

3. What is the source of true happiness?
God alone is the source of true happiness.

4. What must we guard in our pursuit of God?
In our pursuit of God, we must guard our spiritual disciplines, our environment, and our friends.

FOR FURTHER STUDY

Scripture Passages
Read these passages and consider how they enhance the study of the pursuit of God and all that was discussed in this chapter.

- Psalm 101:2–3
- Matthew 6:33
- John 10:10
- John 15:10–11
- Romans 12:1–2
- Galatians 5:22–23
- Ephesians 5:2–6

FAQ #28

 How Do We Demonstrate Our Love For God?

 We must obey His commandments to demonstrate our love for God.

I heard a heartwarming story of obedience not long ago. An acquaintance told me that she and her husband were hoping to catch a few extra winks of sleep one Sunday morning, but they were having great difficulty because the kids were already up and in their parents' bedroom. The parents normally don't let their kids watch a lot of cartoons, but they thought it wouldn't hurt to relax the rule that Sunday morning, so they could get a little more sleep.

My friend and her husband eventually got up and went into the living room where the children were watching a television preacher. She was pleased at their choice, but curious, so she said, "Why aren't you kids watching cartoons?" One of her children said, "We were going to, but when we started to change channels, the preacher said, 'Don't touch that dial!' So we're watching him."

Now that's obedience!

Obedience is a sign of loving God:

■ **John 14:15,** "If you love Me, keep my commandments."

■ **John 14:21,** "He who has my commandments and keeps them, it is he who loves Me."

■ **1 John 5:3,** "For this is the love of God, that we keep His commandments."

When I was coming out of the unhelpful early influences and misunderstandings described above, these verses became a big help to me. I had feared that only those who had a precious, sweet relationship with God were loving Him. Now I realized that I could love God even though I did not have a highly emotional relationship with Him. God does not want us to obey him on the level that we obey a drill sergeant. Rather than with gritted teeth and clenched fists, He wants us to obey him with an open heart and willing spirit, confident that that which He requires of us is for our good:

■ **1 John 5:3,** "For this is the love of God, that we keep His commandments. *And His commandments are not burdensome* (emphasis mine).

■ **John 15:10,** "If you keep My commandments, you will abide in My love; just as I have kept My Father's commandments and abide in His love. *These things I have spoken to you, that My joy may remain in you, and that your joy may be made full* (emphasis mine).

God wants our obedience to flow from trust in His goodness and love for Him.

So how do we obey God from the heart? It is when we come to deeply believe that everything God asks of us is something good for us, something to keep us from harm. Let's look, then, at three things which may keep us from believing that.

Barriers to Obedience: Ignorance

Sometimes we disobey God because we didn't know what is right to do. I got into some uncomfortable debts because I simply didn't understand biblical principles concerning finances. However, even though I was ignorant in that area, I paid a price anyway. Ignorance does not prevent consequences, though you might be tempted to say, "Well, that's not fair for you to pay that penalty if you didn't know what was right. And yet, if we were spared the consequences of sin simply because we were ignorant, I suspect it would make us want to increase our ignorance rather than our knowledge! The fact is, there are certain rules for temporal life, and if you break them you get burned. If you want to go to heaven, you must believe in and receive Jesus personally as your Lord. If you want to live a rich, full life, you must adhere to the principles of living as found in the Scripture. Yet it is possible to obey one set of rules and not the other.

For example, there are church-going non-Christians, there are Mormons, there are New Agers, who follow the principles of living that we find in the Scriptures. As a result, many have fairly happy lives, even though they may not be Christians. On the other hand, there are Christians who are forgiven and redeemed, and headed for heaven, who, for one reason or another, do not follow closely the principles of Scripture, and who are miserable as a result.

Ignorance may prevent our heartfelt obedience.

Our great task, then, is to become a serious student of the Bible in order to believe with the heart that all of God's commands for us are for our good, to spare us unnecessary heartache.

Why Do I Need To Know This?

If I don't understand the role of obedience and emotions in loving God,

1. I am likely to misunderstand what it means to love God. The typical result is to focus on emotional experiences and pay less attention to the importance of obedience to His commands.

2. I may get frustrated and quit trying to love God because we cannot sustain sufficient ongoing emotional experiences.

3. I may never break my commitment to this world and as a result, never begin giving away money, time, and emotional energy to eternal causes.

4. I may never grow in my commitment to love other people.

Barriers to Obedience: Rebellion

Other times when we disobey, we know what is right and are capable of doing it, but we choose the wrong way. That is rebellion.

God deals patiently and compassionately with weaknesses like ignorance, but He deals strongly with rebellion. We see in 1 Corinthians 11 some people coming to the communion observances where they had a small, ceremonial meal, and eating all the food. They were gorging themselves with food that was supposed to be eaten in small measure, and they were not leaving any food for the others to take communion with. In addition, they were getting drunk on the communion wine, and in general, being dreadfully rebellious about an area of behavior which they could easily have controlled. As a result, some of the offenders were weak, and some were sick, and some of them even died. They were judged by God, and the judgment was significant.

Rebellion is a form of disobedience God judges firmly.

Parents know that their two-year-old is just that, and they are willing to deal patiently and compassionately with the child's weaknesses. They acknowledge that and accept it. But with outright rebellion, they have no choice but to discipline the child, as consistently as the rebellion warrants. The same is true with God and us.

Rebellion does not pay. If you are weary of feeling God's hand of discipline, you can repent and be restored to fellowship.

Barriers to Obedience: Lack of Trust

A third reason we don't obey God is that we may not really trust Him. Yet if He is good, loving, and just, then everything He asks us will be for our good. Since all His intentions for us are good, we would be foolish to disobey Him. It would be self-defeating, self-destructive, and counter-productive. When we disobey Him, chances are that we don't really trust His intentions.

When we think of obeying God, too often, we think of tight-lipped, grim-faced endurance of something that we ought to do, but don't want to do—something akin to taking bitter medicine. That is not the way it has to be. When we rest in His character, and power, and intentions, and take His word at face value, we can look forward to obedience. We can take refuge in obedience. We can obey, not with gritted teeth, but with relaxed heart. Whenever we find ourselves gritting our teeth in obedience to God, we are temporarily forgetting, or overlooking, or failing to believe something good and true about Him.

A Boost Toward Obedience: God's Truly Good Purposes

So, let's look at God's intentions for us, in order to confirm that everything He requires of us is for our good. In Deuteronomy 8:1–16, the Lord required the Israelites to obey Him in every situation because He wanted to do good for them in the end. Let us fix this truth in our minds. Even though it is not always easy to do things God's way, or painlessly, it is always right. Just as a surgeon has to "hurt" in order to heal, God must sometimes hurt, or allow hurt, for our own good. Is that a bad intention?

In Deuteronomy 6:24–25 and 10:12–13, we read that God gives us commands for our good. In Psalm 119:67, 71, 75, we see that it was good for David that God sent him trials. In Romans 8:28, we see that everything works together for good to those who love God and who are called according to His purpose. Goodness is God's intention for us. And the genius of God's system is that what He requires is what brings us to our highest good.

O**ur failure to trust God's goodness toward us hampers our heartfelt obedience.**

Does He ask you to be honest? It is for your good. It is harmful to you when you are not.

Does He ask you to be sexually pure? It is for your good. It is harmful to you when you are not.

Does He ask you to be ethical in your business dealings? It is for your good. It is harmful to you when you are not.

Does He ask you to be industrious? Does He ask you to be kind to others? Not to get angry? To be charitable in your finances? To forgive others? To be patient and loving and kind? It is for your good. It is harmful to you when you are not.

Surely, there are other reasons to obey God: out of respect for Him; to be a good testimony to others; to contribute well to society.

But in addition to all other reasons to obey God, it is best for you.

We only fool ourselves by thinking that we can take what we like of His commandments and ignore the others. Not all medicine meant to cure illnesses tastes pleasant. We may refuse to take it, but what will the consequences be? That mindset leads to spiritual malnutrition. It keeps us from the full satisfaction we long for. It condemns us to a half-realized spiritual experience; we see what could be truer in our lives, but we don't experience it. We are half-full glasses of water trying to overflow, and it doesn't work.

God desires five responses from us.

We don't have to be as miserable as some of us are. We don't have to live with as much pain as some of us do. But there is only one way out: His way. Not your way, not half your way and half His way, but His way. Period.

God says "Be ethical in your business dealings." Are you cutting corners because you don't trust that God will take care of you?

You are dating a non-Christian, and people have warned you about it, but you are getting in deeper and deeper. Don't you trust God to take care of you in your loneliness and lack of purpose?

You are head over heels in debt. You are trapped into a lifestyle you can't afford. If one thing goes wrong, it will all come down around your head. But you won't get out. Don't you trust that God is sufficient to satisfy you? Don't you trust God to take care of you?

Don't do it—whatever it is that you are tempted to disobey God in. Stop. Remind yourself who He is. Remind yourself that He only loves you, and wants the best for you. Trust Him. Obey Him. You are the one who will suffer if you don't. And you will be the one to be blessed if you do.

Because it is impossible to keep all of God's commands in the forefront of our consciousness, let's reduce them to the five basic responses God asks of us. When you take all the commands and responsibilities in the New Testament and put them into "like" categories, you will find five responses God wants from us:

1. To Love God

In return for loving Him, He wants to give us a satisfying relationship with Himself, the God of the universe. Everyone would long for spiritual intimacy with God if they knew who He was. He wants us to be deeply satisfied with Him (John 4:24).

2. To Love Others

In return for loving others, He gives us rewarding relationship with others. Our relationships with people help determine our quality of life. Everyone wants friends and a few very close friends. By loving others, we gain many friendships and a few close friends (Philippians 2:1–4).

3. To Esteem Ourselves

When we see ourselves as He sees us, we gain a satisfying relationship with ourselves. Most of us have a love/hate relationship with ourselves. We instinctively love ourselves but hate many things about who we are and what we have done. Yet God wants us to feel good about who we are in Christ, to experience the joy of seeing ourselves as He sees us. We are each priceless. If we believed that, it would free us of poor self-esteem. But no one person is of more value than another. If we believed that, it would free us of pride (Ephesians 1:3–4).

> "When I have learnt to love God better than my earthly dearest, I shall love my earthly dearest better than I do now."
>
> *C. S. Lewis*

4. To Be a Steward

In return for being a steward, God frees us from the tyranny of pursuing "things" for their own sake. We hope that "things" will satisfy. "He who dies with the most toys wins," says the bumper sticker. But things don't satisfy, so God seeks to free us from the trap of living for them. He wants to free us from the bondage and futility and disappointment of living for this world (Ephesians 4:17–24).

5. To Be a Servant

In return for being a servant, God gives us a satisfying purpose in life. Man was not created to live selfishly, for himself only. He was created to live unselfishly, for others. Just as an eagle cannot be happy confined to a cage, so we cannot be happy confined to a life consumed with ourselves. As everyone lives for others, everyone's needs are met in a context of unity and harmony (Ephesians 4:11–16).

From these five examples we see that what He asks of us He intends for our good. When we believe that deeply, it gives us the capacity to obey God with a willing heart, even when the medicine tastes bad.

FAQ #29

 How Must We Treat Our Resources?

 God has given each of us the three basic resources of time, talents, and treasures, and we must commit those resources to Him.

1. Time

You have just as much time as anyone else. And no matter how busy you are, there is always time to do the will of God.

Many of us neglect the will of God because we think we are too busy. We feel trapped by obligations, hemmed in by urgent requests, and overwhelmed by circumstances. Often, however, the way out is merely by rearranging our priorities. If something prevents us from doing God's will it is something that needs to be given up. We demonstrate our love for God by giving Him the time we should.

2. Talents

Each of us has been given spiritual gifts and personal abilities that God wants us to use for His glory as well as for our own pleasure. Yes, the things God has gifted us to do are things we enjoy doing. Many of us are not enjoying life as fully as we could be because we are not doing what God gifted us to do. It may be something for ministry, such as helping, or teaching, or counseling, or giving. It may be something like paint-ing, or writing, poetry, or cooking, or something else. When we use our gifts and talents to His glory we receive personal pleasure. We can demonstrate our love to God by using our gifts and talents for Him.

3. Treasure

God has given each of us a per-sonal treasure in our money. It is God who gives us the ability to make a living, and in some cases to prosper. Out of what He enables us to earn, He wants us to give some of it back to Him. Why? Because He needs the money? Not if He is the One who created silver and gold. Why, then? Because he uses it as a test to determine what we are living for. Are we living for self only, or are we living for God and the expansion of His king-dom? If the latter, we will manifest it by giving to that kingdom gener-ously.

So, the one who loves God is the one who gives of His resources of time, talents, and treasures.

> God has given each of us three precious resources: time, talents, and treasures.

FAQ #30

 How Must We Treat Others?

 How we love others is a test of how we love God.

In Matthew 22, someone in the crowd asked Jesus what the great-est commandment was. Jesus said it was to love the Lord your God with all your heart and with all your soul and with all your might. Then, he said that the second greatest commandment is like it. It is to love your neighbor as yourself.

Perhaps the best known principle in the Bible is the Golden Rule:

"Do to others as you would have them do to you" (Luke 6:31 NIV). This is one of the most powerful sentences ever heard by man. It is the single-sentence answer to the majority of the suffering of mankind. First John 5:1–2 says, "Whoever believes that Jesus is the Christ is born of God, and everyone who loves Him who begot also loves him who is begotten of Him." First John 4:10–11 states, "In this is love, not that we loved God, but that He loved us and sent His Son to be the propitiation for our sins. Beloved, if God so loved us, we also ought to love one another." Finally, we read in 1 John 4:21, "And this commandment we have from Him: that he who loves God must love his brother also." The final test of loving God is that we love others.

THINKING BACK

There it is. It is inescapable. Who loves God? The one who obeys His commandments. The one who gives out of his God-given resources. And the one who loves others. In isolating these three aspects, I hope we have de-mystified what loving God means. It is not being swept up regularly by emotion, feeling warm fuzzies toward God all the time.

When feelings toward God come, that is certainly not to be despised. But sometimes you feel it, and sometimes you don't. Loving God, therefore, is about doing the right thing regardless of your emotional state.

Loving others is evidence that we love God.

In *Loving God*, Chuck Colson tells the penetrating story of a Russian doctor named Boris Kornfeld who was condemned to a concentration camp in Siberia because, as a Jew, he could not profess primary allegiance to the Soviet state, even though he was a confirmed socialist. The degrading and inhumane treatment at the prison camp stripped him of everything, including his idealism about socialism and his personal faith in God. Nevertheless, he met up with a Christian in the camp who shared Christ with him as the Jewish Messiah, and Kornfeld believed.

As a camp physician, Kornfeld had to sign death certificates for prisoners who were killed by the savage treatment they received. But on the certificate he was forced to say they had died of natural causes. Because of his faith in Christ, he finally refused to lie, and as a result the guards plotted his death. Kornfeld realized this, but having accepted the probability of death, he felt free to live. He signed no more papers or documents sending men to their deaths. He no longer participated in the evil system. And soon he realized that the anger and hatred and violence in his soul had vanished. He wondered whether there lived another man in Russia who knew such freedom!

Kornfeld longed to tell someone else about this new life of obedience and freedom. One gray day, Kornfeld began spilling his story to a cancer patient on whom he had operated. The patient missed the first part of the story because he was drifting in and out of the anesthetic. But Kornfeld's enthusiasm held the patient's attention, though he was shaking with fever. All through the afternoon and late into the night the doctor described his conversion to Christ and his newfound freedom. The patient knew he was listening to an amazing confession. Though the pain from his operation was severe, he hung on the doctor's words until he fell asleep.

The young patient awoke early the next morning, but the doctor did not come. During the night, while the doctor slept, someone had crept up beside him and dealt him eight blows on the head with a plasterer's mallet. The doctor was dead. But his testimony did not die. The patient pondered the doctor's last, impassioned words. As a result, he too became a Christian. He survived that prison camp and went on to tell the world what he had learned there. The patient's name was Alexander Solzhenitsyn (pp. 27–34).

Kornfeld was not going to lie, and he was going to testify for Jesus. Here was a Christian who, in the face of terrible odds, loved God from the heart. Ready to die for love of God, he shows us how to live out of that same love.

SPEED BUMP!

Slow down to be sure you've gotten the main points of this section.

1. How do we demonstrate our love for God?
We must obey His commandments to demonstrate our love for God.

2. How must we treat our resources?
God has given each of us the three basic resources of time, talent, and treasures, and we must commit those resources to Him.

3. How must we treat others?
How we love others is a test of how we love God.

FOR FURTHER STUDY

Scripture Passages

- Psalm 90:12
- Matthew 25:15–28
- 2 Corinthians 9:6–7
- 1 Timothy 3:3
- 1 Timothy 6:10
- Hebrews 13:5
- 1 Peter 4:10

Read these passages and consider how they integrate with your understanding of loving God.

FAQ #31

 How Do We Reconcile Pain and Suffering with God's Character?

 We recognize that there are spiritual realities that transcend our comprehension.

Pain Is Universal

All people in all times everywhere have suffered. Certainly, some people have easier or harder lives than others, but suffering has always been a part of the human experience. This is true from the most primitive and godless cultures to the great people of the Bible. Joseph suffered terribly. So did Moses, David, and Daniel. So did Paul and James. What about Jesus? It should come as no surprise to us when we suffer. "Affliction does not come from the dust, nor does trouble spring from the ground; yet man is born to trouble, as the sparks fly upward" (Job 5:6–7).

We Lack Information

We can also assume there are reasons for our sufferings that we are unaware of. We may have to admit that we simply don't know. This goes back to the question of why God allowed sin to enter the world in the first place. That question has never been answered adequately. But since God is all good, there must be an explanation which we cannot fathom. There are many things about God that we are too little

> "Madame," I said, "if our God were a pagan god or the god of intellectuals—and for me it comes to much the same—He might fly to His remotest heaven and our grief would force Him down to earth again. But you know that our God came to be among us. Shake your fist at Him, spit in His face, scourge Him, and finally crucify Him: what does it matter? My daughter, it's already been done to Him."
>
> *George Bernanos*
> *Diary of a Country Priest*

to carry. We just don't have all the information, or we don't have the ability to understand.

There are millions of things I don't understand. For example, I cannot read a computer manual. I work on a computer all the time, but the only thing I can do is word processing, which is virtually "nothing" compared to what computers will do. People who fully know computers live in an entirely different world than I do. I will never forget the time I crashed my hard drive. This was the rough equivalent of hitting my computer on the head very hard, so that it forgot everything it ever knew. I had given it the wrong command, and it erased its memory. It first even asked me if I was sure I wanted to do that. But I was out in the ozone somewhere and said, "Yes."

Obedient monster that it is, it immediately obliged and erased everything it knew. It forgot that I had ever entered and stored anything in its memory. I had two entire books I had written in the memory, as well as a lot of important information concerning the church I was pastoring.

We often lack satisfying information about our suffering.

The screen went blank. I typed some stuff, and the screen remained blank. My computer was in a coma.

The effect on me was dramatic. I sat there in stunned silence trying to comprehend the significance of what had happened. For some time I was unable to admit that it had happened. Surely there was some way out of this. But, no. I had crashed my hard drive.

I left my office for a meeting where others were waiting for me. I lumbered into the room, slumped into my chair, and groaned the unthinkable, "Men, I've crashed my hard drive." A tense silence filled the air. Then someone ventured to speak. "Maybe you haven't lost everything. Maybe you have just lost the ability to get to everything." That is like saying, "Maybe your computer is not in a coma. Maybe it just has amnesia which a good doctor can correct." So I phoned the good doctor, "Magic Phil," who restored my hard drive. In several hours and for $250, the memory was back.

I wish I could explain to you how this man restored my computer, but I can't. I sat and watched him a while. Without a computer manual, he typed stuff that looked like "swearing" in the Sunday cartoons. No words—just hieroglyphics. I say "without a computer manual" because to me it is like saying that he typed from memory the first twenty pages of the phone book.

I go to the lengths of telling this story, because it illustrates the fact that there are people who are far above us in intellectual power, and yet they are still human. There are people who know things that we will never understand. Maybe your weakness is literature, or plane geometry, or physics. The people who send rocket ships to the moon or who operate on the human brain are intellectually above the rest of us. Yet they are still only human. If there are humans who dwarf us intellectually, why should we be surprised if God dwarfs us intellectually? There are things which God knows, which make sense to Him, which we don't know or can't understand.

We cannot fully understand what God is doing with us.

How many times have you been puzzled by something, only to have it resolved later? You smack your forehead with the palm of your hand and say, "Ooohhhh. Of course." I am convinced that, when it comes to unexplainable suffering, the first sound most of us will hear in heaven is our hand smacking our forehead followed immediately by the surprised cry, "Ooohhh! Now I see!"

When on earth we cried, "Oh, God, when I was hurting, why didn't You heal me? When I was suffering, why didn't You come to my aid? When calamity was coming my way, why didn't You hear me? When I was alone, why didn't You visit me?" When we get to heaven, we will pause momentarily, and say, "Oh. Now I see." For now we must assume that there is yet some information, some understanding, which we don't have.

We Lack Intellectual or Spiritual Ability

Next, we must accept that our ability to comprehend is limited. Let me tell you another story about Sugar Bear (please forgive me. She was just such a good source of illustrations). When she was about six months old, we began to try to train her. The first command was "Come." The book said that you were to say, "Come," and if she didn't come, you were to go get her and bring her to where you were when you said "Come" and that you were to do that in an enclosed space until she learned to come to you every time. Then you were to graduate to an open space. I don't know if that was the best way, but it did work.

However, at first, Sugar Bear didn't understand what it was all about. She was intimidated by this change in her routine and this limitation on her freedom. She got apprehensive and insecure, and thought that we were unhappy with her. Her eyes clouded over and she became immobile. She feared the whole world.

"Why are they doing this? What have I done? Why don't they like me anymore?" her eyes seemed to be saying. We continued to love her and work with her, and the day came when she learned not only that command, but every other command which we needed for peaceful co-existence.

After she learned what we wanted and was reassured that we still loved her, everything was OK. But until that time, she was very unhappy. We had tried to explain to her: "This is not going to hurt you. We aren't angry with you. This is for your own good. This will make your life safer and better, and improve our relationship." Nothing mattered. She wanted out. Given the option, Sugar Bear would have bailed out of the learning process without a second thought. But we cared for her too much to let her. So we worked with her, and pushed through the apprehension and insecurity, and the result was a dog that was safer, more pleasant to be around, and had a better relationship with us. She was raised to a higher level of canine existence because of us.

Of course, the point is obvious. God works with us. But we cannot understand what He wants, or what He is doing. We get apprehensive and insecure. We may even get a little rebellious, as Sugar Bear did from time to time. We just don't have the ability to understand all that God is doing with us. But if we let Him, God will keep working with us, to push through the barrier, and raise us to a higher level of human existence.

We Must See Things From God's Point of View

While we cannot know all that God knows regarding our suffering, we can, however, learn to see things from God's point of view. God does not want to be your genie in a bottle. He does not want to be your cosmic vending machine. He does not want to be the solution to your equation. He wants a relationship with you. He wants you to know Him and to love Him. He has created the world so that nothing in our Christian life will work very well unless it forces us to deepen our relationship with Him.

Prayer won't reduce to an equation. Understanding how to live the Christian life won't reduce to an equation. Finding God's will won't reduce to an equation. If you are not doing what you can to get to know Him, paying attention to your successes and failures, learning how He works, and getting to appreciate Him, it won't work.

We can learn to see things from God's view.

To understand what God is up to, we must go back to original creation. God describes in profound understatement what He did, in stages, and, after each stage, said, "It is good." When He finished with all the stages, He said, "It is very good." In Job we read, "The morning stars sang together and all the angels shouted for joy." Proverbs continues the buoyant mood: "I was the craftsman at his side. I was filled with delight day after day, rejoicing always in his presence, rejoicing in his whole world and delighting in mankind."

"Oh, that their hearts would be inclined to fear me and keep all my commands always, so that it might go well with them and their children forever!" God cries. "Oh, Jerusalem, Jerusalem," Jesus lamented, "How I have longed to gather you to My self as a hen gathers her chicks under her wings, but you refused Me!"

God longs for an encounter with us. He longs for a relationship with us. He longs to know us and have us know Him. He longs to be intimately related to us. He longs for us to love Him, and to believe him, and believe in Him, and follow Him. In response, He promises untold blessings. Typically, like an undisciplined child or untrained dog, we won't follow Him completely enough, long enough to taste the blessings.

We get frustrated, or the pain gets too intense, and we begin to resent God. We clench our fists and grind our teeth and squint our eyes in rebellion. Why doesn't God fix our problems?

We have not yet begun to see things from God's point of view. From God's point of view, He is not out to get us, nor is He out to neglect us. He is out to make us like Him, and for reasons hidden deep in the mysteries of His will, He allows and uses pain.

God our Savior fully experienced the pangs of human suffering.

However, God is not unaware or unaffected by our suffering. He does not leave us to suffer alone. He is not regaling the departed saints in a celestial party, oblivious to our plight, waiting for the day when we will finally join them. Rather, God is with us, always. When we hurt, God hurts. He feels our pain. He takes in all our pain. In some mysterious way, a God who is complete and lacks nothing links Himself with our suffering.

When it comes to God's identifying with our suffering, I have always felt that Jesus had credibility, because He came to earth and suffered for me far more than He asks us to suffer. So when He asks me to suffer, while I may not enjoy it, He has credibility with me. The Bible teaches that Jesus delighted to do the Father's will, but He did not delight to go to the cross. Scripture says that Jesus "endured the cross" (Hebrews 12:2). Luke 22:44 indicates that in the Garden of Gethsemane, Jesus was in emotional agony, and sweat profusely. Hebrews 5:7 says He cried. He asked for the help of friends who deserted him in Mark 14:32. He had to have angelic assistance to continue (Luke 22:43). Again in Mark 14, He said, "My soul is overwhelmed with sorrow to the point of death." So if Jesus asks anything of me, I feel a sense of fraternity with Him.

But I confess to struggling with God the Father. It always seemed unfair to me for God to be up in His celestial glory, untouched by the ravages of sin in the world, telling me to be patient, that it would all be over some day, and we'd get our reward.

However, as I searched the Scriptures, I discovered how wrong I was and how I missed the fact that anything Jesus the Son experiences is also experienced by the Father. God feels our pain. He takes it into His own heart. When we hurt, God hurts. Not only does he feel pain for us, but for all those on earth; and not only all those on earth, but all those who have ever been on earth, and all those who will be on earth. Those of you who are parents know how much pain you go through watching your children hurt. When they are in physical or emotional pain, your heart breaks with them. In the same way, God hurts when He sees us hurting.

Scripture says, "God was in Christ reconciling the world to Himself" (2 Corinthians 5:19). Where is God when it hurts? He is on the cross, taking to Himself in Christ the pain, agony, and terror of all the suffering of all the world for all time. As believers, we are united with Christ. When we suffer, God the Father suffers. When we are in pain, God feels and hears and cares.

No, God does not escape. He has chosen not to escape. Even from heaven, when I hurt, God hurts, and so I no longer cry out, "God, why don't you make it stop hurting?" He is hurting with me. In fact, we must not fail to marvel at how God's coming to us in Jesus the Son is the most potent way God could and did drink deeply from the bitter waters of human suffering. And so there must be a reason for suffering which lies beyond me.

God identifies with our suffering as the Creator who grieves over sin's carnage.

I have been struck so many times when a parent takes a child to visit the doctor or dentist and the child either fears pain or feels pain. The child cries out from the bottom of his soul when the parent hands the child over to the doctor. Yet when it is all over and the doctor hands the child back to the parent, the child does not recoil from the parent for handing him over to such pain. Rather, sensing that there is some higher good, and sensing that the parent is hurting even as the child hurt, the child grabs the parent's neck, and buries his face into his shoulder, and at last is comforted.

We must try to see our suffering from God's point of view. He cares. He hurts with us. He obviously would prefer that we not suffer and promises that there will come a day when we will not suffer. But for reasons hidden in the mystery of His will, He has allowed suffering to come into creation…but with the suffering, He suffers, too.

FAQ #32

 How Do We Deal with Our Personal Pain?

 We must believe that our suffering matters.

We know, then, that our suffering matters to God. For instance, there is purpose behind it. In Hebrews 12:5–9, we read:

My son, do not regard lightly the discipline of the Lord, nor faint when you are reproved by Him; for those whom the Lord loves He disciplines, and He scourges every son whom He receives. It is for discipline that you endure; God deals with you as with sons; for what son is there whom his father does not discipline? But if you are without discipline, of which all have become partakers, then you are illegitimate children and not sons. Furthermore, we had earthly fathers to discipline us, and we respected them; shall we not much rather be subject to the Father of spirits, and live? (NASB).

Yet there is a level on which we cannot see or know the reason. We cannot understand. When suffering comes on that level, we must trust, by faith, that it matters to God.

In his book *Disappointment With God*, Philip Yancey writes about the "Great Wager." The Book of Job, Yancey wrote, is more than a book on suffering; it is a book about faith, the heart of which is the Great Wager in chapter 1. Satan wagers that if God takes away all blessing from Job, Job will curse God. God allows the wager. Yancey wrote:

When people experience pain, questions spill out—the very questions that tormented Job. "Why me? What's going on? Does God care? Is there a God?" This one time, in the raw recounting of Job's travail, we, the onlookers, not Job, are granted a view behind the curtain. What we long for, the pro-logue to Job provides: a glimpse into how the world is run. As nowhere else in the Bible, the book of Job shows us God's point of view, including the supernatural activity normally hidden from us.

Why Do I Need To Know This?

1. If I don't know this, I may think that I am alone when I wrestle with why God doesn't relieve human suffering.

2. I may think there is something dreadfully unspiritual about myself if I'm angry with God about suffering.

3. I may feel alone and abandoned by God when I personally suffer.

4. I may not have a way of relieving the intellectual tension created by unexplainable suffering.

5. I may not realize that I need to study the life of Jesus to gain a better perspective on how to go through suffering.

6. I may not know how to appropriate the grace of God during times of trials.

> Job has put God on trial, accusing him of unfair acts against an innocent party. Angry, satirical, betrayed, Job wanders as close to blasphemy as he can get—just to the edge. But Chapters 1 and 2 prove that, regardless of what Job thinks, God is not on trial in this book. Job is on trial. The point of the book is not suffering: Where is God when it hurts? The prologue dealt with that issue. The point is faith: Where is Job when it hurts? How is he responding? (165)

> Yes, there was a wrestling match in Job, but it was not between God and Job, it was between God and Satan, although, most significantly, God had designated the man Job as His stand-in. The first and last chapters make clear that Job was unknowingly performing in a cosmic showdown before spectators in the unseen world (p. 168).

Elihu, one of Job's accusers, said, in essence, "Job, you must have sinned terribly to have brought this suffering down on your head." Elihu was flat wrong, however. The opening and closing chapters of Job prove that God was greatly affected by the response of one man and that cosmic issues were at stake.

Our suffering matters.

"The 'Wager' offers a message of great hope to us all," Yancey concludes. "Perhaps [it is] the most powerful and enduring lesson from Job. In the end, The Wager resolved decisively that the faith of a single human being counts for very much indeed. Job affirms that our response to testing matters. The history of mankind—and, in fact, my own individual history of faith—is enclosed within the great drama of the history of the universe" (p. 170).

The Bible hints that something like that may be happening to us when we suffer. The suffering which we go through which makes no sense to us all is perhaps a cosmic drama in which we are not alone, though in our pain we feel very much alone. Perhaps at that moment when we feel most alone, most abandoned, perhaps at that very moment the eyes of heaven and hell are focused most sharply on us, to witness our faith and the triumph of God's grace. Thus, when we feel most removed from reality and purpose, we may be the most involved in them.

Sometimes God does give us a glimpse behind the veil. In my book *30 Days to Understanding the Christian Life*, I wrote about a lady in a church I pastored. Her husband, a school teacher, had applied for the unusual position of going into space aboard a NASA space shuttle. He had all the prerequisites. He was bright, well educated, an excellent communicator, a popular teacher, and so on. Their excitement grew as they envisioned that he might be the first non-astronaut in space. From the wife's point of view, it was not even really the possibility. It was the probability. There was no one more qualified than her husband.

While their hopes were at their highest, they were abruptly and cruelly shattered. A technicality beyond their control prevented getting the extensive application in on time. In the most favorable scenario, it would be one day late. No, there could be no extension; no late papers, as it were. No, they would not be granted an exception. No, he would not be the first non-astronaut into space, not because he was not qualified but because the application would be one day late.

The lady who told me this story was crushed, devastated, angry with God. It was a bone that stuck in her throat. She couldn't get over it until the day of the launch, that is. Watching the Challenger on television lift off and surge into that brilliant, cloudless blue sky, she said aloud, "That could have been my husband. God, how dare you!" The moment the words passed her lips, the Challenger exploded in a ball of flame, divided like a huge smoke wishbone, and dropped lifelessly to the ocean below. Everyone on board had died. She fell backwards onto her bed, shaken to the core.

We are not usually given glimpses behind the scenes like this. But it strikingly helps us see that there is more going on than meets our eye. What we see is not all there is. Our thoughts do not encompass all information. Therefore, we must always hope in God, and trust His actions, His timetable, His providence.

When you suffer, take strength. Take encouragement. Your life matters. It counts. God knows you. He loves you. He has not abandoned you. You are not alone. When you hurt, He cares. When you are lonely, He cares. When you are confused and fearful, He cares. He is not off in a corner of the universe paying attention to something that really matters. He is living within your heart, calling and hoping that your faith will remain strong in the struggle. And, He promises to set all things straight one day. What a celebration that will be!

FAQ #33

 How Is Jesus Our Example in Suffering?

 Jesus set the example of total trust and obedience to God, even in suffering.

We can look to Jesus for an example of how we can endure suffering. When He was on the cross, he cried out, "My God, My God, Why hast Thou forsaken me?" This is a quote from Psalm 22:1–3:

My God, my God, why has Thou forsaken me?
Far from my deliverance are the words of my groaning.
O my God, I cry by day, but Thou dost not answer;
And by night, but I have no rest.
Yet Thou art holy,
O Thou who art enthroned upon the praises of Israel (NASB).

In this remarkable passage, we see the psalmist David, crying out prophetically, because he feels utterly forsaken. He says that both day and night he cries out, but God does not answer him. Yet without any explanation for God's silence, the psalmist affirms the holiness of God: "Yet, Thou art Holy."

Ultimately, our suffering may drive us to only this confession. We are free to cry to God. We may get no relief. We may get no answer. Yet God is still holy.

Again, Jesus provides an example for us as recorded in 1 Peter 2:20–24:

For this finds favor, if for the sake of conscience toward God a man bears up under sorrows when suffering unjustly. For what credit is there if, when you sin and are harshly treated, you endure it with patience? But if when you do what is right and suffer for it, you patiently endure it, this finds favor with God. For you have been called for this purpose, since Christ also suffered for you, leaving you an example for you to follow in His steps, who committed no sin, nor was any deceit found in His mouth; and while being reviled, He did not revile in return; while suffering, He uttered no threats, but kept entrusting Himself to Him who judges righteously; and He Himself bore our sins in His body on the cross, that we might die to sin and live to righteousness; for by His wounds you were healed (NASB).

Jesus simply took it, trusting in God to get Him through it, and trusting that in the end all would be well. No matter how hard, God will see you through it, and in the end all will be well. Trust also sustained the martyrs whose sufferings are described in the remarkable book, *Foxe's Book of Martyrs*. It tells story after story of early Christians who were martyred for their faith. Hebrews 11 says the world is not worthy of such people. In the providence of God, He calls some to higher degrees of suffering than others, and in the end, when all suffering for God's people will end, they will stand before the Lord and the hosts in heaven, and it will be declared to all the celestial hosts, "The world was not worthy of them!"

SPEED BUMP!

Slow down to be sure you've gotten the main points of this section.

1. How do we reconcile pain and suffering with God's character?
We recognize that there are spiritual realities that transcend our comprehension.

2. How do we deal with our personal pain?
We must believe that our suffering matters.

3. How is Jesus our example in suffering?
Jesus set the example of total trust and obedience to God, even in suffering.

FOR FURTHER STUDY

Scripture Passages

- Romans 8:18
- 1 Corinthians 12:26
- 2 Corinthians 4:16–18
- Galatians 3:4
- James 1:2–4
- 1 Peter 2:20–24
- 1 Peter 4:13

Read these passages and consider how they integrate with your study of the problem of suffering.

FAQ #34

How Do We Cling to God When It Hurts?

When we are in pain, we must trust the Scriptures and use the pain to force us closer to God rather than drive us farther from Him.

Three common circumstances often force us to cling to God. The first is during terrible physical or emotional pain. It may be the physical pain of disease, or from an accident, or even deep nausea or just a hard to describe terrible feeling. It is a great cross to bear. Or it may be emotional pain, like the pain of fear, or anger, or bitterness, or loneliness, or rejection, or disappointment, or black unrelenting depression.

Sometimes, physical or emotional pain gets so intense that the only thing we can do is cling to God. As we saw above, in the Garden of Gethsemane Jesus was in horrible anguish about His death. What level of emotional pain would it take to cause the body to sweat great drops of blood? Apparently that happens when deep emotional stress causes the capillaries near the surface of the skin to rupture, and blood, perhaps mixing with perspiration, came sweating out.

Pain forces us to cling to God.

The apostle Paul had some kind of problem which we don't fully understand. In 2 Corinthians 12:7–10, Paul described something which he calls a thorn in the flesh and a messenger from Satan to buffet him. Was it a physical malady, or was it spiritual suffering? My guess is both, perhaps a physical ailment caused by demonic attack. Whatever it was, Paul prayed three times for the Lord to remove it. The Lord didn't remove it. He simply said, "My grace is sufficient for you."

> "God weeps with us so that we may one day laugh with Him."
>
> *Jürgen Moltmann*

If God's grace is sufficient for Jesus and Paul, I would have to say that it is also sufficient for us as we tread life's troubled waters. Our measure of grace may not at times be enough for us to go water skiing but simply to keep our nostrils above the surface. Or, if we sink below the surface, it will be enough to bring us back up to keep from drowning. In fact, many people testify about times when His grace did not seem to be sufficient, but later they admitted that it was.

Biblical characters clung to God.

My wife and I have a friend who was in labor with her first child for nearly twenty-four hours. She was in the hospital most of that time in terrible physical anguish, which began to affect her emotions and mental stability. Suddenly she jumped out of bed and began throwing her clothes into her suitcase. Her husband yelled, "Susan! (Not her real name.) What are you doing?" She said, "I've had it. This is ridiculous. It is unreasonable to think a person should have to go through this, and I am not going to do it. I'm going home!"

Well, it took some persuading, but she got back in bed, had the baby, and eventually was able to laugh about it. But at the time, it was not funny. The pain and emotional distress became so great she cracked. It did not seem like the grace of God was sufficient for her. Yet, here she is, alive and healthy, and so is her child. The grace of God was sufficient for survival. But not for "Easy Street."

The Psalmist cried to God in Psalm 22:

My God, my God, why hast Thou forsaken me? Far from my deliverance are the words of my groaning. O my God, I cry by day, but Thou dost not answer; And by night, but I have no rest...I am poured out like water, and all my bones are out of joint; My heart is like wax; it is melted within me. My strength is dried up like a potsherd, and my tongue cleaves to my jaws; and thou dost lay me in the dust of death (verses 1–2, 14–15, NASB).

In this intensely intimate cry of the soul, we see the psalmist simply clinging to God. There is no railing against God. There is no questioning. It is simply the cry in the night of a hurting and fearful child to his parent. Sooner or later, help will come. In the meantime, there is nothing to do but cling to God.

To cling to God when it hurts, in spite of the pain, is to keep on trusting. You cry for relief. You find means of grace for easing the pain from any legitimate source, such as medication or mental exercises for physical or emotional pain, the help of friends, good books to read, solitude or forms of diversion. Prayer, of course, should be a constant. Through it all, you cling to God.

FAQ #35

 How Do We Cling to God When We Are Spiritually Dry?

 We must believe that the drought will eventually end and we must continue to be faithful to the spiritual disciplines.

A second time we must cling to God is when we go spiritually dry. Just as sun spots are said to cause a sixty-year cycle of drought in the cornfields of Indiana, so there seem to be cycles of spiritual drought in the lives of Christians.

These droughts may be minor periods of spiritual dustiness, or they may be major league droughts,

Why I Need to Know This

1. If I don't know this, I may think that there is something wrong with me for not being able to escape my pain or deal more effectively with it.

2. I may feel that I would be better off if I just had more faith.

3. I might do exactly the wrong thing in trying to deal with my suffering.

4. I might be tempted to give up when there is still hope.

when the soil of the soul dries and cracks like fissures on the desert floor. During periods of dryness, we must do at least three things, we must acknowledge that the dryness is not permanent. Rain will come again. Life and growth will return. God has not forgotten you. Remember what Jeremiah said: "This I recall to my mind, therefore, I have hope. The Lord's lovingkindnesses indeed never cease, for His compassions never fail. They are new every morning; Great is Thy faithfulness. The Lord is my portion. Therefore, I have hope in Him." Keep on believing that the drought will end. It will.

Your spiritual drought will end.

Second, be on guard for things you may do to bring on the spiritual drought yourself. Insurance companies put out stress evaluation surveys to rate a person's chance of getting sick. If you have certain things happen to you, you rate them with a numerical value and then total them up to see what your overall stress impact is. For example, if you have moved recently, that equals so many points. If a loved one has died, that is so many points. If you have been physically ill for more than a week, so many points, and so on. A financial setback, a divorce, a change of jobs, all of these have stress values, and after going through the entire survey you add up your total to see the likelihood of getting sick from stress.

According to that chart, I should have died two Christmases ago. Circumstantial turmoil takes its toll and induces, in many instances, spiritual dryness.

Other factors which directly affect your spiritual vitality are: how many hours you work, how much sleep you get, whether you smoke, drink alcohol, drink coffee or other caffeinated beverages, how balanced your diet is, and how much exercise you do. Monitoring your lifestyle can give significant insight into things that might tend to induce spiritual dryness.

Third, pay attention to spiritual disciplines. When under prolonged intense suffering, we can sometimes lose our grip on spiritual disciplines like prayer, meeting with Christian friends, counseling, Scripture reading, even the laying on of hands by elders.

In his book *The Spirit of the Disciplines*, Dallas Willard writes:

We can become like Christ in character and in power and thus
realize our highest ideals of well-being and well-doing. That is
the heart of the New Testament message. We do it by following
him in the overall style of life he chose for himself. If we have
faith in Christ, we must believe that he knew how to live. We
can, through faith and grace, become like Christ by practicing
the types of activities he engaged in, by arranging our whole
lives around the activities he himself practiced in order to
remain constantly at home in the fellowship of his Father. What
activities did Jesus practice? Such things as solitude and silence,
prayer, simple and sacrificial living, intense study and meditation
upon God's Word and God's ways, and service to others.

We must develop a counterculture mentality. by which I mean
that we embrace a lifestyle different than the world's.

For example, our culture does not put a premium on solitude,
rest, prayer, or meditation. Thus in his book *Ordering Your Private
World*, Gordon MacDonald has written:

I get the feeling we are a tired generation. Evidence of that
fatigue abounds in a multitude of articles about health problems
related to overwork and exhaustion. Why is there so much
exhaustion and fatigue today? One reason is that we are not
following the biblical view of rest. Resting properly is a key to
ordering our private worlds. Rest was not meant to be a luxury,
but a necessity. By rest, I do not mean amusement. Although
[amusements] may provide a sort of momentary rest for the

body, they will not satisfy the deep need for rest within the private world.

Again, the psalmist wrote about his own time of spiritual dryness. In Psalm 63:1, we read, "O God, my God, I shall seek Thee earnestly; my soul thirsts for Thee, my flesh yearns for Thee in a dry and weary land where there is no water."

When David was spiritually dry he simply told God that he was spiritually dry. But we see from his worship, even then, that he clings to God. Notice Psalm 63:2–3 and 6–8:

Thus I have beheld Thee in the sanctuary, to see Thy power and Thy glory. Because Thy lovingkindness is better than life, my lips will praise Thee...When I remember Thee on my bed, I meditate on Thee in the night watches, for Thou hast been my help, and in the shadow of Thy wings I sing for joy. My soul *clings* to Thee; Thy right hand upholds me (emphasis added, NASB).

David got so spiritually dry that all he could do was tell God and cling to Him. But in the clinging, he was faithful to worship, pray, and meditate.

What do you do if you are so spiritually dry that you don't want to worship, pray, and meditate? I think you should tell God how you feel and do the best you can. You don't have to experience happy emotions in order to love and cling to God. You can simply say, "As an act of love, manifested by my simple obedience, I offer you my prayer. I offer you my worship. I don't feel that I am getting anything out of it, but it means something to me to know that it is a way of demonstrating that I really do want to love You."

So let us remember that we can cling to God by doing three things. First, realize that the drought is not permanent. It will end. Second, try to bring the circumstances of our lives under control, so that we are not bringing spiritual dryness on ourselves unnecessarily. Third, do what we know we should do of the spiritual disciplines even when we don't feel like it. It is an act of love to God which He will reward.

FAQ #36

 How Do We Cling to God When We Don't Know What to Do?

 We must cling to truth, counsel, and wisdom, believing that God is leading us even when we discern no evidence of it.

A third time when we must cling to God is when we have lost our way—when we don't know what to do. We don't know what God's will is, and yet we have to do something. Or at least we have to decide *not* to do something.

How many times have you had to make a decision, perfectly willing to do God's will, but without any real confidence that you knew what God's will was? If you are like a lot of us, you have done it many times. But often the situation is more difficult than just a quick decision. You would like to change jobs, but it would require a move out of state, and such a move would be hard on your family. What do you do? Or, you would like to get married, but have not met anyone you feel comfortable marrying. You can't imagine that God wants you single the rest of your life, but neither can you imagine marrying anyone you currently know. You might do some things to try to meet others, and yet you feel a little funny about that. What do you do?

This is a time to cling to God. At times you will know the will of God only when you look backwards. At times you simply will not know what to do, and yet you will be forced to make a decision anyway. Cling to God. Trust Him. Count on Him to be faithful to you and to His word, to lead you even though you don't feel led.

THINKING BACK

In the book *Adrift*, Steve Callahan tells the story of sailing the Atlantic Ocean, not far off the coast of Spain, when his sailboat was destroyed. At the last instant, he was able to salvage his life raft and a few emergency items. Amazingly, he drifted until he landed on a Caribbean island. It is a compelling story of endurance and determination.

As I read the book, I was struck with the relationship Callahan had with his life raft. When the seas were calm, he took little notice of his raft. He would even jump out of it and swim around, taking the raft for granted. But when the winds picked up, he would think seriously about his life raft. He would wonder if it would hold him. He would contemplate his raft, investigate it, even feel gratitude for it. But when the sudden and violent storms that stalk the Atlantic in the summer would swoop down on him like a hawk on a hapless chicken, that is when his relationship with the raft was the purest. He didn't jump out of the raft and swim around, nor sit and contemplate it. Rather, he wedged himself deep down inside his raft, buried himself in it, and clung to it until the storm is over.

When we feel adrift in the sea of life, when we feel at the mercy of circumstances around us, God is still our raft. In the easy times, we may take our raft for granted. We might even jump out of it and swim around lazily, gazing at our raft from a distance. But when the winds pick up we find ourselves wanting to get in our raft. We think about God. We investigate Him, we analyze Him, we ponder him. But it is during the storms of life that our relationship with God may be at its purest. We bury ourselves in the deepest recesses of God that we know, and we simply hang on until the storm is over.

We also have an advantage with God that Steve Callahan didn't have with his raft. God has promised to never leave us or forsake us (Hebrews 13:5). Are you hurting? Do you cope with physical pain, or are you burdened with emotional pain? Are you going through a spiritually dry time? Do you feel adrift, uncertain, confused? Do you feel at the mercy of circumstances? Cling to God. Listen to His promises:

Trust in the Lord with all your heart, and do not lean on your own understanding. In all your ways acknowledge him, and he shall direct your paths (Proverbs 3:5–6 NASB).

Cast your burden on the Lord, and he will sustain you (Psalm 55:22 NASB).

He will cover you with his feathers, and under His wings you may seek refuge; His faithfulness is a shield and a bulwark. You will not be afraid of the terror by night, or of the arrow that flies by day; of the pestilence that stalks in darkness, or of the destruction that lays waste at noon. A thousand may fall at your side, and ten thousand at your right hand, but it shall not approach you (Psalm 91:4–7 NASB).

The Lord liveth, and blessed be my rock and let the God of my salvation be exalted (Psalm 18:46 NASB).

Take God at His word. Say to yourself that no matter what comes I will cling to God: I will cling to my conviction that He will somehow see me through, even though there are times when it looks impossible. Mother Teresa once said something like, "When we get to heaven, our suffering on earth will be little more in comparison than a bad night in a cheap hotel."

SPEED BUMP!

Slow down to be sure you've gotten the main points of this section.

1. How do we cling to God when it hurts?
When we are in pain, we must trust the Scriptures and use the pain to force us closer to God rather than drive us farther from Him.

2. How do we cling to God when we are spiritually dry?
We must believe that the drought will eventually end and continue to be faithful to the spiritual disciplines.

3. How do we cling to God when we don't know what to do?
We must cling to truth, counsel, and wisdom, believing that God is leading us even when we discern no evidence of it.

FOR FURTHER STUDY

Scripture Passages
Read these passages and consider how they relate to clinging to God.

- Psalm 22:1–3
- Isaiah 40:27–31
- Lamentations 3:1–28

FAQ #37

 What Is True Worship?

 True worship is the complete offering of our complete selves to God.

Several Hebrew and Greek words in the Bible are translated "worship." But there is only one main Hebrew word for "worship" in the Old Testament and one main Greek word for "worship" in the New Testament. Both mean the same thing. Yet it does not mean "to sing," or "to gather together in a congregation," or "to go through a ceremony," or even "to get quiet and solemn." The word "to worship" literally means "to prostrate oneself, to fall down on one's face."

I admit that I was surprised by that. I don't think the word must always be taken literally. It can also mean, in a figurative sense, to spiritually prostrate oneself before God.

Does that puzzle you, as it did me? What is intended by a word that means "to prostrate oneself"? When we prostrate ourselves figuratively before God, what are we doing? If we don't understand that we may not know what it means to worship.

True worship equals a total commitment.

Let's imagine what would be going on in our hearts and minds if we prostrated ourselves before someone else. If I prostrated myself before someone, I would be recognizing his authority. I would be affirming his superiority. I would be demonstrating my submission. I would be placing myself at his mercy and disposal. It would be a massive gesture of total personal

> "A man can no more diminish God's glory by refusing to worship Him than a lunatic can put out the sun by scribbling the word 'darkness' on the walls of his cell."
>
> *C. S. Lewis*

offering and sacrifice. In the land of the free and the home of the brave, in the land where all men are equal, in the land of rugged individualism, we can hardly imagine prostrating ourselves like that. But if we did, we would be saying by our body language that "You are greater than we are, and we recognize that. We humble ourselves before You, place ourselves at your mercy and disposal, and agree to do anything You tell us to do.

Disciplining ourselves for personal worship is difficult but rewarding.

So, when the Bible uses the word "worship" it means more than we may have thought. In John 4:23–24, we read, "an hour is coming, and now is, when the true worshipers shall worship the Father in spirit and truth; for such people the Father seeks to be His worshipers. God is spirit; and those who worship Him must worship in spirit and truth" (NASB). To paraphrase, God seeks people who will give themselves to Him totally. He is seeking people who will say, "You are greater than I am, and I recognize that. I humble myself to You, I place myself at Your mercy and disposal, and I agree to do anything You tell me to do."

Is that what you do on Sunday mornings? Worship, in its fundamental meaning, is an offering of the complete self to God. Unless we understand that, we will misunderstand both what we do in worship and what God requires. As a result, we will miss the deep and meaningful relationship with God that we long to have.

FAQ #38

 How Do We Worship God Personally?

 We worship God personally by making a total life commitment to Him.

Do you have a regular, satisfying time of worshiping the Lord alone? You are in a minority if you do. Many people find it almost impossible to develop any regularity at daily devotions with the Lord.

Why is that? One reason is that we have trouble disciplining our-selves to do anything regularly. We have trouble exercising, we have trouble dieting, we have trouble keeping our car clean and well main-tained. A second reason is that we are so busy. A third reason is that we don't get anything out of our time with God. We are faithful spending time with God on a daily basis for a few days or weeks, but eventually rigor mortis sets in, we stiffen up, and our quiet times are gone.

The reason? One reason is that nothing excites us consistently. Our first Fourth of July fireworks show probably mesmerized us. Now, we take it in stride.

Another reason, as has been mentioned, is that we are not yet a great audience. Our minds have become so secularized and so trivial-ized that our tastes no longer enjoy great things. How, then, do we develop a taste for great things? In the chapter on pursuing God, we recognized that we can change what our taste buds enjoy, but only after a time of tastelessness, during which we must simply "tough" things out. We can lessen our taste for sugar and heighten our taste for healthy foods by cutting down on sugar and eating more healthy foods, but the healthier foods will not be as enjoyable to us at first.

The same thing is true mentally, emotionally, and spiritually. On a personal level, we must cut out our spiritual sugar, and begin con-suming more spiritually healthy things so that we can develop a taste for great things. When we develop a taste for greater things, we have a greater appreciation for God and His Word.

You are making a choice when you fill your mind with the trivial, the sensual, and the violent. You are alienating yourself from God. So, if you want to begin appreciating God, you must eliminate mental and spiritual junk and poison from your diet.

Whenever I make these kinds of com-ments, I always get a few charges of "legal-ism." It is no more legalism to state these dangers clearly than it is to warn of the physical dangers of too much sugar, or too much cholesterol, or too much caffeine.

Worshiping God on a personal level is not a matter of spending a few minutes with Him and a

Bible and a daily devotional book. It is a matter of total life commitment. It is a matter of prostrating yourself before Him spiritually, and all that that means, 24 hours a day. Worshiping God cannot be compartmentalized.

FAQ #39

 How Do We Worship God With Others?

 We worship God with others by coming to Him in a spirit of true worship, and then engaging in activities designed to publicly give God the worth due Him.

Finding a church that you are happy with in which to worship is a big deal. There is no one church that can satisfy all Christians, just as there is no one restaurant that can satisfy all patrons. Our tastes

Why Do I Need to Know This?

1. If I don't understand that worship is a total commitment of my life, I may believe that worship is only a religious activity.

2. I might not understand that religious activity is important only if it is founded on a total commitment of one's life to God.

3. I might believe that worship activities are passive "shows" which I attend, rather than opportunities for me to participate in from the heart.

4. I might not understand that to fail in the pursuit of meaningful worship is to miss out on a fundamental responsibility and opportunity for God's blessing.

differ, so one church will be best for one person, and another church will be best for another person. In addition, one church may meet our needs for a number of years, but as we grow older, our perspective and values might change, and so we may feel a need to find another church. That is perfectly understandable and perfectly acceptable.

Many of us believe (I confess that for a long time I held this idea) that when you come to a worship service you are coming to an event which other people put on for you. You are a spectator and other people are the performers—the musicians and the preacher particularly. Worship, then, becomes entertainment, and the goal is often to be moved emotionally. I now understand that that is incorrect. In true worship, God is the audience, the congregation acts, and the worship team, including the minister, helps the congregation to participate. Worship, therefore, is active, not passive. It matters whether or not we participate.

Church worship focuses our acts on the audience—God.

Also, if worship is a matter of prostrating one's self before God, it is not necessary to be moved emotionally every time. It is more important that the mind be engaged than that the heart be moved.

Again, worship is the spiritual prostrating of ourselves before God. In church worship this would include the acceptance and affirmation of biblical truths, perhaps through public readings, songs, and prayers. It is declaring to God the wonder of who He is and what He has done.

Many people are not moved by traditional hymns and "higher" music. That is why I believe that balancing the two can bring a greater strength than only one or the other. You can sing some choruses and then some traditional hymns. In special music, sometimes it can be more contemporary and sometimes more traditional. This creates a good balance, a more complete act of worship, than if we insisted on one or the other.

Church worship is not all singing. Nor is it all preaching. If all we did were to sing a hymn, pass the plate, and listen to fifty minutes of preaching, we might be having a grand Bible study, but many of us would not be worshiping. Bible teaching tends to leave the audience passive, and worship must be active. Balance—that is the key. We must balance the activities of singing, prayer, and affirming creeds and statements of faith with listening to special music and preaching.

FAQ #40

 How Can We Become Better Worshipers?

 We can become better worshipers by making worship a higher priority.

It is easy to get confused and substitute other things for worship. Many years ago Thomas K. Beecher once preached for his brother, Henry Ward Beecher, at the Plymouth Church in Brooklyn, New York. Henry was a famous preacher, and many people had come to hear him. When Thomas stood up to preach, some people began to move toward the doors. Realizing that they were disappointed because he was substituting for his brother, Thomas raised his hand for silence and announced, "All those who came here this morning to worship Henry Ward Beecher may leave now. All who came to worship the Lord may remain."

It happens to us, doesn't it? We go to church not because God is there but because a certain preacher is there, or a certain choir or vocalist. There is nothing wrong with enjoying good preaching and music, but those are only aids to worship. God is why we worship. We have to be sure we are getting it right.

I think there are four steps to begin cultivating a capacity for great worship:

1. Decide to care about worshiping Him. Many of the things we value in life we decided to value. We must value worship of God. We must sit back and ask ourselves: what is important to me? What do I want to live for during the rest of my life? And then, we must decide to include worshiping God.

2. **Fill your life with great people.** The easiest way to become different is to hang around people who are like how we want to become. So hang around them. Ask them over for dinner. Go to a concert with them. Ask them over to your house for conversation. Take them boating on the lake or something else, anything else, but spend time with them. And then, talk about spiritual things. Go below the surface. Transcend news, weather, and sports. One of Margie's and my favorites is to ask people how they became Christians. Or something else might work for you. But fill your life with great people.

3. **Fill your life with great pursuits.** Find something noble to do, and do it. Do one thing, if one is all you have time for. It might be helping cancer patients. It might be visiting prisoners. It might be teaching children's Sunday school. It might be teaching adults how to read, or becoming a really good usher or something else, but fill your life with great pursuits. Of course, the only way you will have time is to drop off the trivial things that keep you from great pursuits.

4. **Fill your mind with great thoughts.** Read things that build you up. Talk with people who challenge you. Watch selectively movies or television shows that encourage you to be a better, bigger person. Think. Carve out time for solitude and quiet, so that your mind can find its true equilibrium. I don't think a person can live a balanced Christian life unless he has adequate amounts of time alone where it is quiet. Write. Keep a journal. Correspond with edifying friends. Fill your mind with great things.

As you do these four things you will become a greater audience and worshiping God will become a more meaningful part of your life. If we remind ourselves that worship does not depend on emotions, we can experiment with things that work for us, changing our procedure often, if that is helpful, and then we can develop a satisfying life of personal and church worship.

Every Sunday morning, something goes on that is a highlight in my life. I worship together with other like-minded Christians. Take away my speaking engagements, my travel, the books I've written—take them all away. But don't take away my Sunday morning worship, and don't take away my every-morning and every-evening time with God. If you don't feel this way already, you can. Be patient. It will take time. But meaningful personal and church worship can be yours.

SPEED BUMP!

Slow down to be sure you've gotten the main points of this section.

1. What is true worship?
True worship is the complete offering of our complete selves to God.

2. How do we worship God personally?
We worship God personally by making a total life commitment to Him.

3. How do we worship God corporately?
We worship God corporately by coming to Him in a spirit of true worship, and then engaging in activities designed to publicly give God the worth due Him.

4. How can we become better worshipers?
We can become better worshipers by making worship a higher priority.

FOR FURTHER STUDY

Scripture Passages

- 1 Chronicles 16:28–29
- John 4:20–24
- Romans 12:1–2
- 1 Corinthians 14:25
- Revelation 4 & 5

Read these passages and consider how they integrate with your study of worship.

BIBLIOGRAPHY

Barclay, William. *The Letters to Galatians and Ephesians*. Philadelphia: The Westminster Press, 1958.

Davies, P.C.W. "The Tailor-made Universe," *The Sciences*. May-June, 1978, 6–10.

Hoyle, Sir Fred. "The Big Bang in Astronomy," *The New Scientist*. Nov., 1981.

Jastro, Robert. "God's Creation," *Science Digest*. Special Spring Issue, 1980.

Lewis, C.S. *A Grief Observed*. New York: The Seabury Press, 1961.

_____. *The Weight of Glory and Other Addresses*. Grand Rapids: Eerdmans, 1965.

MacDonald, Gordon. *Ordering Your Private World*. Nashville: Oliver-Nelson, 1985.

McGrath, Alister. *Understanding the Trinity*. Grand Rapids: Zondervan, 1988.

Morely, Patrick. *The Man in the Mirror*. Nashville: Thomas Nelson, Inc, 1989.

Ortlund, Anne. *Up With Worship*. Ventura, CA: Regal Books, 1975.

Ostling, Richard. "Kingdoms to Come," *Time*. Special Issue, Fall, 1992.

Packer, James I. *Concise Theology*. Wheaton, IL: Tyndale, 1993.

Pascal, Blaise. *Pascal's Pensées*. W. F. Trotter, trans. New York: E. P. Dutton, 1958.

Sullivan, Deidre. *What Do We Mean When We Say God?* New York: Doubleday, 1990.

ten Boom, Corrie. *The Hiding Place*. Uhrichsville, OH: Barbour and Company, 1971.

Weaver, Kenneth. "The Incredible Universe," *National Geographic*. May, 1974.

Willard, Dallas. *The Spirit of the Disciplines*. San Francisco: Harper & Row, 1988.

Yancey, Philip. *Disappointment With God*. Grand Rapids: Zondervan, 1988.